Future Gaming

Part of the Goldsmiths Press Future Media series

This series offers short, sharp interventions in response to short-term, utilitarian and instrumentalist thinking about media and technological futurism. Our emphasis on feminist, queer, trans, anti-racist and/or speculative approaches to media and technological futures calls for alternatives to TED thinking.

Future Gaming

Creative Interventions in Video Game Culture

Paolo Ruffino

Goldsmiths
Press

© 2018 Goldsmiths Press
Published in 2018 by Goldsmiths Press
Goldsmiths, University of London, New Cross
London SE14 6NW

Printed and bound by Clays Ltd, St Ives plc
Distribution by The MIT Press
Cambridge, Massachusetts, and London, England

Copyright © 2018 Paolo Ruffino

A CIP record for this book is available from the British Library

Library of Congress Cataloging-in-Publication Data
Names: Ruffino, Paolo, author.
Title: Future gaming / Paolo Ruffino.
Description: London, England; Cambridge, MA: Goldsmiths Press, [2018] |
    Includes bibliographical references and index.
Identifiers: LCCN 2017035594 | ISBN 9781906897550 (hardcover : alk. paper)
Subjects: LCSH: Video games – Social aspects. | Video games – Moral and ethical aspects.
Classification: LCC GV1469.34.S52 R84 2018 | DDC 794.8–dc23
LC record available at https://lccn.loc.gov/2017035594

ISBN 978-1-906897-55-0 (hbk)
ISBN 978-1-906897-67-3 (ebk)

www.gold.ac.uk/goldsmiths-press

Goldsmiths
UNIVERSITY OF LONDON

A Benedetta

Contents

Introduction: Creative Game Studies

The video game industry is experiencing an identity crisis. Until recently, industry experts, journalists and gamers were confident about describing the medium. Producers and players of video games were assumed to have similar and predictable habits and interests. Video games were marketed as forms of entertainment, and their future was bound up with the development of computing technologies and graphics accelerators. However, the most elementary notions about the industry and culture of digital gaming now appear less simple to analyse, and this generates contradictory descriptions of players, designers and critics.

Until a few years ago, video games were allegedly made by white, male, geek programmers for an audience of the same class, race, gender and education. Nowadays, video games are being played and produced by unpredictable groups and categories of people, who until recently would never have been associated with digital gaming (Anthropy 2012; Juul 2010).[1] The physical boundaries of game technologies and the ownership of both hardware and software are becoming controversial issues, as hacking, modifications, patches and upgrades contest the limits and uses of video games. The history of the medium has been described in textbooks on the topic as a straightforward progression of technological inventions (Herz 1997; Poole 2000; Kent 2001). However, studies on the origins of the medium have revealed that the current technological landscape was at

---

[1] Even former US Defence Secretary Donald Rumsfeld has made his own video game: Churchill Solitaire. As reported in the *Wall Street Journal*, 22 January 2016, Churchill Solitaire was the favourite card game of British Prime Minister Winston Churchill, who used to play it in his spare time during World War II. Donald Rumsfeld, as the article reports, has managed to develop a digital version of Churchill's game despite not having any programming skill.

least partly determined by chance events, and that its early stages were largely influenced by military investments (Huhtamo 2005; Huhtamo and Parikka 2011; Crogan 2011; Suominen 2016). Furthermore, video games are no longer just games, as their use is now widespread in sectors such as education, health and, thanks to the gamification movement, self-improvement and productivity (McGonigal 2011; Deterding et al. 2011; Fuchs et al. 2014).

What are video games? Who plays them? Who makes them? What are they for? Answering these questions is no longer a straightforward task. The response given so far to the identity crisis has been to reaffirm the same old answers to the new questions, as if looking back to the past in search of safe and stable notions could reassure us that nothing will ever change dramatically. The denial consists not in hiding the new dynamics of the game industry and culture, which are quite evident, but in preserving the structures of discourse surrounding the medium: allegedly, the new actors, practices of play and modalities of production of games might appear different, but they are consistent with those of the past. In fact, most of these recent changes might not be as new as they are imagined to be. Most of these allegedly new practices that now require original responses from those involved in the industry have always been present but have received little or no attention, probably because of the destabilising effect that the emerging questions bring with them.

For example, it is often claimed by experts that the previous stereotypical male gamer is now being replaced by a new category of consumer, that is, the women who play video games on consoles, smartphones and social networks, and by more casual consumers of various ages. However, women have always been present in video game culture, but their presence was mostly treated as an exception to the rule (Nooney 2013). Video games today are often produced by single individuals or small groups of people rather than large companies, in what is known as the phenomenon of independent gaming. But similar modalities of work have been dominant for more than two decades, particularly in the United Kingdom and other parts of Europe; what is currently known as independent game development might just be the name given to the reappearance of pre-existing modes of production under a new spotlight and in different geographical contexts (Foddy 2014). The events surrounding the hacking of PlayStation Network discussed in this book have also offered the opportunity to redefine who has the authority to decide about the ownership, legitimate uses and physical and temporal limits of a video game console. While in the past this position was occupied by the console manufacturer, many commentators argue that it should now be taken by those who buy the console. However, it is not because of the emergence of Internet connection and digital distribution that hardware and software are becoming malleable in the hands of their users: forms of reappropriation and modification have been dominant in the definition of video game subcultures since the early years of the medium (Carbone and Ruffino 2014).

The shorthand answers given so far to the identity crisis of the industry have a double effect. First, they acknowledge that something is changing, that the old actors who dominated gaming culture might be replaced by or go along with new ones, and that the development, distribution and marketing of video games uses a variety of tools that did not exist before. Secondly, they preserve our knowledge about the past, present and future of video games, and provide reassurance that the discourses produced so far have always identified the key issues and major tendencies and might just need an update. In short, even if some practices and phenomena have been overlooked, it is still possible to *tell the truth* about video game culture. However, these answers are only strategic and partial, and they neglect that the crisis might concern the very possibility of articulating the truth about video games and their players.

Future Tellers

On closer inspection, most of these concerns can be grouped together as broader questions about the future of the medium. The imagined evolution of the medium of the video game has mostly been presented through narratives of technological progression, and questions about the future have long been dominant when discussing the improvement of technologies for digital gaming. The video game industry is organised around a series of events that predict, explain and illustrate its own future. Since 1995, the gaming industry has had its own trade show, the Electronic Entertainment Expo, also known as E3. The event usually takes place in

Los Angeles, California. E3 gives the video game industry a separate space from the other trade shows on electronic and digital products, such as CES (Consumer Electronics Show), where it was previously hosted. But E3 is not just a display of the current products of the gaming industry; it is mostly a showcase of what is yet to come. Presentations, slogans and announcements to the press all evoke the future, the imminent next stage in a process of constant upgrade and update of video game titles, the 'evolution' to be 'experienced', as the main title of E3 2015 suggested (Entertainment Software Association 2015).

Events such as E3 signal crucial moments in the yearly schedules of the main video game companies, and well-received presentations can positively influence the stock market rates, particularly for major publishers such as Sony, Microsoft, Valve and Nintendo. However, it is not just during the three days of Californian heat that the future of the gaming industry is discussed. The industry appears to be structured by the very idea that the future needs to be narrated almost constantly. Video game magazines, since their origins around the 1980s, have been publishing previews and speculations on the games to be released. These might be imminent game products as well as projects set to appear in one or more years from the time of writing. Occasionally the games previewed are later cancelled or dismissed by their publishers and never hit the shelves, thus becoming elusive games that many have seen, in pictures and videos, and no one has ever played (Ruffino 2012).

The promises of the industry leaders and the predictions of the journalists are not the only contexts in which the medium of the video game is discussed in the future tense. Particularly in recent years, digital games have been the object of a re-evaluation in terms of their social acceptance and potential for bringing changes in our lives. Previously seen as a dangerous medium, capable of corrupting a generation of teenagers, now video games are presented by private and public institutions as a tool that could be used to improve our health, education and social and political lives, boost the economy and, occasionally, achieve artistic accomplishments (Carbone and Ruffino 2012). On these occasions, what video games can do is always seen as projected in an imminent future.

Since 2010, for example, there have been proposals that video games could fix the world. This is how Jane McGonigal introduced her TED Talk

(McGonigal 2010). McGonigal presented on stage her plan for solving any problem of our species by gathering the energies spent by gamers while playing their video games. Her proposal is simple: if so many gamers put so much effort into solving trivial issues while playing games, what might happen if their collective intelligence was channelled towards real-life problems? In her view, the problems of the planet could be reduced to design problems, and game design, so successful in attracting millions of players, could prove useful in structuring solutions that are appealing and engaging for many.

In the future, video games will be used to 'save the real world together' (McGonigal 2011, 296–344). Through video games, we will solve global warming and oil crises, find medical cures for viral diseases, and be happier in general. This is what McGonigal believes, as well as many other design and marketing consultants. The practice of using game design techniques in serious contexts has been named gamification, and it is now a widespread concept for online and digital businesses (Deterding et al. 2011; Fuchs et al. 2014). In these contexts, gamification is presented as a useful technique for attracting and retaining new customers by engaging them in game-like scenarios and challenges. These are supposed to create affiliations with brands and encourage gamers to share their activities in the games with friends and contacts, who might also become new consumers (Zichermann and Cunningham 2011).

Stories around the potential of the medium have also attracted those who believe that games could be used for social purposes and activism. These current positive discourses on the medium have influenced the position of several public institutions in the United States and in many European countries. During the Computer Science Education Week in December 2013, in what soon became a popular speech among communities of gamers, US President Barack Obama invited students to not 'just play a video game' but also to 'make one' (De Loura and Paris 2013). The speech was part of a longer series of direct appeals promoting a wider adoption of computer science in educational programmes. Previously, Obama's administration also promoted the use of video games to 'solve problems' (Gaydos 2012). In March 2011, Obama invited the students of the Tech Boston Academy to 'be stuck on a video game that's teaching you something other than just blowing something up' (Lee 2011). The video game industry is here seen as being capable of generating jobs (ones that academic institutions should act to prepare students for) and, at the same time, fostering the cultural production of a nation.

In a similar fashion, in March 2012, the British chancellor George Osborne secured tax breaks for the video game industry in the UK, and Richard Wilson, representative of trade body TIGA, reacted positively, stating that: 'by making this announcement, the government has recognised that games are culturally as important as films . . . The second thing is, it will mean a massive financial boost to the games sector – we should see £188m of investment expenditure because of this proposal' (Stuart 2012). The European Union has also been investing in video games as technologies for fixing the future. In the Horizon 2020 funding scheme, 'Gaming and Gamification' is one of the many areas to which public and private institutions can apply. The scope of the funding is to 'mainstream the application of gaming technologies, design and aesthetics to non-leisure contexts, for social and economic benefits', as 'gaming and gamification will not only create new solutions and methodologies to address societal issues, but it will also help . . . to seize new business opportunities' (European Commission Research and Innovation 2016).

Despite the period of uncertainty that surrounds the medium, there are political and financial actors that promote video games as instruments to achieve a brighter future. In the future, video games might save us all and be used to improve our health care, economy and culture. What, then, is the problem?

Promises, Promises

These and other similar promises about the future of gaming do not accord with the problematically shifting scenario that the medium is currently facing. As consolatory narratives they do not work very well. In fact, these stories about the medium only hide the complexities of the problems they seek to resolve, and are reassuring for many precisely because they do not change anything. To explore this further I will take as an example an online advertisement which is apparently celebratory of the medium.

The *In the Future* campaign commissioned by international bank HSBC to the agency JWT Dubai, released in January 2013, looks at video games as one among many examples of how the bank could foster the businesses of the future (JWT Dubai 2013). In the video, the protagonist Emir, a young man from Istanbul, is making a video game called *Sticky Weasel*. In the plot of the advertisement, the game suddenly and unexpectedly reaches worldwide popularity, with people everywhere in the world playing it on their mobile phones. The boy decides to protect the trademark, merchandise the game and further expand the brand. Ultimately, *Sticky Weasel* inspires the production of a film and Emir goes to Hollywood, where he is interviewed on the red carpet at the movie's premiere. All this happens thanks to HSBC, which guarantees funding of the project and helps the game attain popularity in a global market. In the final scene, Emir's mother stops her son from working and reminds him it is time for dinner, which probably reminds the viewers that HSBC is a global bank that preserves local values, as is repeated in their slogan, and provides financial assistance to anyone with a good business idea, regardless of their social and economic background.

This and the previous examples are not just paradigmatic of the wide popularity reached by a new and positive understanding of the medium of the video game on the part of political and financial organisations. They are also examples of the contradictions and of the rather repetitive nature of the stories that are usually told, by industry experts and commentators, about the things that gamers can now do with video games, and that games can do for gamers. The allegedly liberating and innovative effects of the technological and social evolution that awaits us are moderated by the not-too-subtle confirmation of existing economic and power relations. HSBC reminds viewers that for each Emir, or any other self-made, one-person company and independent entrepreneur who accepts President Obama's suggestion to make games, there must be a significant investment that makes that dream possible and guarantees a safety net in case of failure.

Moreover, the advertisement does not mention that the independent game development scene, to which it implicitly refers, does not feature, at the time of writing, any significant game developer from Turkey,[2]

---

[2] I could only find one example: TaleWorlds Entertainment, an independent video game company based in Ankara, Turkey. Indeed, while there may be exceptions, these mostly confirm the trend. Festivals and conventions on independent game development have been trying to broaden the geographical perspectives of the scene. The A Maze festival, established in 2008, has organised events on independent games in Germany, South Africa, Romania, Palestine, Russia, Croatia, Kosovo and Cuba, in the hope of challenging the Western-centric views of other institutions.

or, for that matter, from any other country where the game industry is not already advanced (that is, the United States, Canada, the United Kingdom and Europe). The message is clear: anyone can make a video game, as long as he or she is already equipped with the same education, technical competency and financial security and is enmeshed in the same cultural context as the old actors of the video game industry. In these promises around the potential of video games, with certain regularity, a denial of the inequalities and difficulties that prevent their fulfilment can be seen. Moreover, these visions of the future work to reinforce the same economic, political and social conditions of the present. The alleged democratisation of the development tools that should now allow anyone to make and publish a video game has in fact failed to appeal to any significant group of people that was not already sufficiently educated and competent to work in the game industry in the first place. Not coincidentally, Obama's speech was addressed to students who can afford both college education and economic uncertainty, two non-negotiable requisites for anyone who wishes to attempt a career in gaming.

Research Reveals That. . .

Interest from political institutions in the potential of digital games starts even earlier than the Obama administration. As pointed out by Jennifer Whitson and Bart Simon, the American National Security Agency (NSA) had already expressed interest in digital gaming as a new context in which to operate massive surveillance and political propaganda (Whitson and Simon 2014). In December 2013, when Edward Snowden released leaked NSA documents from 2007 and 2008, video games and virtual environments appeared in the reports of intelligence operations, and their utility as an 'interactive influence medium' was also debated. An entire chapter on the 'exploitation and function of games' has precise directions for security agencies and shows how and why these should pay attention to the current developments of the video game industry. The NSA offers three main reasons for looking at digital games. First, the new tools of production make video games easier to manufacture and release, thus allowing large portions of the population to potentially make their own game. Second, video games are popular among the American population and globally, and it is suggested in the document that the 18–35-year-old-male audience category might still be the most involved in the consumption of games. Finally, games can be used for political propaganda, to influence public opinion, and for military recruitment and training. In the concluding chapter, titled 'Winning hearts and minds *virtually*', the NSA makes explicit suggestions about how the medium can be used both to promote American values and to counter controversial propaganda. Also, the NSA outlines strategies for exploiting online gaming to collect intelligence data on players and control communications within the game (Whitson and Simon 2014, 310–11).

From the NSA's point of view, the future of gaming does not look very playful. In fact, the future looks rather disheartening, filled with inequalities and injustice, and at the service of the same ideologies and authorities that frame the current political and economic scenario. This future looks very similar to the present; mostly, I argue, because the voices that are telling us about the future (the main publishers who gather at E3, HSBC, the NSA and the other aforementioned institutions from within and outside the game industry) are the same ones that are currently shaping the present narratives around the medium. From these points of view, it is certainly comforting to narrate a future that confirms and reinforces the conditions of the present.

Narratives of the future involve statements about technology, finance, education and politics, all areas which are looked at from the safe standpoint of data-driven research. It is quite helpful to look at the sources used to justify these visions of the future. The NSA leaked document explains that most of the ideas around 'Games and Virtual Environments' have been collected over the course of one year of research of 'academic journals and papers, newspaper and magazine articles, textbooks, non-fiction works, in-game exploration and personal interviews on games, psychology and sociology [*sic*], as well as attendance at seminars on these issues (for example the Serious Games Conference or SAIC's Cyber-Influence Conference series)' (ProPublica 2013). The Serious Games Conference, for instance, offers insights to business, educational and political institutions about the uses of games in non-playful contexts, while SAIC is a company which specialises in security and surveillance for governmental, military and commercial institutions. The report by the NSA is thus based on sources that are expected to convey a safe and reassuring confidence in the facts around technologies and video games. The document is, after all, nothing more than a comforting overview which reassures its readers that terrorism can and will be defeated thanks to a detailed understanding of the present and the future of the medium.

In a similar fashion, Jane McGonigal and other gamification evangelists never forget to mention numbers and facts about the supposedly beneficial effects of video games. On McGonigal's personal website a page is significantly titled 'SuperBetter: Show Me the Science!'[3] Here one finds a collection of all the links to the research supporting McGonigal's online game SuperBetter, a game where players give themselves a real-life goal and are guided through it by a step-by-step series of actions, involving mental, physical and social exercises. The tasks are allegedly based on scientifically proven facts, and the website offers an overview of the key academic publications that have inspired the game (it also suggests that 'we can get even more science' by buying the book).

The problem with using facts, data and statistics is that these are presented with the pretence of explaining how things are and how they will be, by repeating the *research reveals* mantra as a *passe-partout*. The problem does not lie in research itself, although of course research might be inaccurate and is surely partial and limited, but rather in its use as a reference to hide the presence of the speaker. The act of revelation is problematic, because it hides the hands that are lifting the veil, and the purposes for which the revelation is enunciated in the first place.

Katherine Hayles, while debating the role of narratives in framing research into artificial life, has argued against

those who maintain that scientific inquiry transcends culture, that it does not matter where or by whom it is carried out or in what cultural contexts it is embedded. Even positing this view of transcendent science requires that one tell a story, in

---

[3] The 'science' is available at: http://janemcgonigal.com/2014/01/06/superbetter-show-me-the-science/ (last accessed 28 July 2016).

this case a story about how science tells truth and about how truth is the same no matter who says it.

Hayles (1996, 162)

Evidence and facts about video games are presented in a variety of circumstances, but it matters where, when and by whom these truths are expressed.

If the medium of the video game is experiencing an identity crisis and a period of uncertainty, then the scientific analyses and reports are like tranquilliser pills for the readers: they may provide calm and comfort, but they only postpone the problem. As argued by Marshall McLuhan, one of the first narcotisation effects of media on bodies and brains is the false idea that these are tools separated from view, rather than things to be deeply involved with (intellectually, bodily and neurotically) (McLuhan 1964).

As an old proverb states: 'when a wise man points at the moon, the imbecile examines the finger.' I believe that the position of the imbecile should be re-evaluated: I would like to ask why the moon has been pointed at, by whom, and from which position of authority the man has been defined as 'wise.'[4] Imbeciles are often playful and, for this reason, in this book I intend to *play with* the future of gaming. I will be staring at the finger, and will push it around to point in different directions that could offer new and different ways of understanding the medium.

Creative Game Studies (or, How to Do Things with Microsoft Word)

This book will *not* offer a guide to the future of video games. Stories about the future of video games are already abundant and their predictions are rarely successful. This book will instead offer an overview and a critique of how the future of the medium is being constructed at the present time, and argue how it could be narrated differently.

As a response to the confidence of the NSA, political administrations, financial groups and visionaries of the future of digital technologies,

---

[4] For a detailed analysis of the old saying, this conversation on Reddit is quite exhaustive: www.reddit.com/r/quotes/comments/2o4e3y/explanation_required_when_a_wise_man_points_at/ (last accessed 29 January 2017).

who draw extensively on truthful, data-based, explicatory accounts of the medium, I will offer a personal and partial perspective on the future of digital games. I believe this could be a useful method to address the identity crisis of gaming: not by offering supposedly more correct answers but by embracing and accepting the persistence of a point of view when talking about the future, the present and the past. The identity crisis will never be fixed, but it is possible to go along with it by looking at the contemporary discourses around video games, resisting the temptation of being too confident about our knowledge of the medium and introducing more temporary theories and strategic readings.

The identity crisis will be approached in this book by way of inventing alternative ways of enjoying the crisis itself or, in other words, a mode of *playing with* video games. I believe that I am involved in this crisis as much as many other gamers and scholars, but I would like to see what can be learnt from it, and whether it could be enjoyable. For this reason, I have a direct proposal for those who study and play within video game culture. My project is called Creative Game Studies and, as I will outline, it offers a mode of writing about and intervening in game culture which is *intuitive, timely, performative, ethical, anti-authoritarian* and *anxious*. Before explaining this definition, I want to avoid possible misinterpretations and explain why a new mode of writing is needed now, and by whom.

The use of the adjective *creative* might raise concerns. Creativity is one of the most common keywords used to define the intellectual and (im)material labour of the contemporary generation of workers involved in the fashion, music, film and game industries. As Angela McRobbie notes, creativity in these contexts usually means little more than having ideas and being competitive, typically at the expense of those who are already socially disadvantaged, and it has been used to frame the concept of the creative industries, where the over-individualisation of workers makes social critique impossible and produces gendered practices of self-exploitation and self-blame (McRobbie 2001, 2016). In the context of this book, creativity means something quite different, although it can be seen as a response to the emergence of the term in contemporary work practices. Creativity is used here to imagine a modality of work for those involved in the study of the medium of the video game. However, in a practice where 'having ideas' is already the norm, what else could creativity introduce?

Creative Game Studies aims at introducing, in the study of video game culture, Kember and Zylinska's appeal for a creative study of media, one that strives to be inventive, critical and performative, and which asks the epistemological question of how knowledge could be produced differently; a theory that embraces the ethico-political responsibility of creating, and that is not afraid to fail (Kember and Zylinska 2012, 173–205). What I take from their proposal is the attention to language and its fabulatory and world-making function, and the notion of creativity (understood through the Deleuzian reading of Bergson) as the creation of something new, or the making of (new) differences. Creative Game Studies intends to critique and create video game culture through a series of interventions and inventions of new differences.

The differences that concern me the most are those that generate new temporalities. Writing does not just take time; it also produces knowledge of time. For instance, the narratives of technological progression promoted by industry leaders have an immediate effect of producing a fragmented vision of time. The introduction of a new game console is often described as belonging to a new generation of products. In the jargon of hardware manufacturers, the release of consoles is divided into historical ages, often associated with the kind of processor used: the 8-bit and 16-bit era of Nintendo historical home entertainment products has been followed by Sony's PlayStation, the bestselling 32-bit console, and then by the Nintendo 64 (named after its 64-bit processor), and so on, until the contemporary generation of the PlayStation 4 and Xbox One, usually referred to as the eighth generation or cycle (the amount of bits is now considered less relevant and generations are conventionally numbered progressively). Likewise, Sony Computer Entertainment has been promoting the vision of Gaming 3.0 as a leading concept for its business in the last decade (Radd 2007; Krotoski 2008). According to Sony executives, Gaming 3.0 follows the 1.0 era of the early home consoles and the 2.0 era of online gaming. In the first two ages, video game products remained unmodified by players after their purchase. Gaming 3.0 focuses instead on the personalisation of the gaming experience, on continuous updates and, more importantly, on the user rather than the developer as a key figure in the production of new content within the game.

These stories differentiate the past, present and future of video games, but in doing so they also put the medium in a repetitive progression. The invention of similar linear narratives is not just to be found in the industry but is often replicated by gamers, commentators and journalists. On most occasions, narratives of technological progression are presented through writing. Throughout this book I will also introduce interventions made via other means: through the design of games (Chapter 2), by becoming hosts of other games and gamers (Chapters 1 and 5), hacking games and consoles (Chapter 3), digging in the desert (Chapter 4), and speaking in a legal trial (Chapter 3). However, video game culture is predominantly based around practices of writing: press releases, tweets, coding, reviews, previews, interviews, and so on. Even YouTube videos require at least an approximate script before being shot, and their significance is partly dependent on the quantity and quality of the written comments they receive.

The writing of stories such as Gaming 3.0 and the fragmentation of consoles into cycles of development offer a *teleological* vision, one that sees a linear and continuous development of technologies for digital gaming. These stories proceed from the past towards the future and through the present. The very idea of the future is grounded on the obsession with newness that pervades not only the video game industry but most hi-tech media sectors. New products are not just important for marketing talk, they also serve to replicate a temporal narrative in the understanding of media and their relation to society and culture.

Teleological narratives also confine technologies to *black boxes*, often equivalent to the products sold on the market, to be periodically replaced by new, better, boxes. The users of these constantly updating technologies are similarly thought of as confined to imaginary boxes within which they can either use technologies or be influenced by them. Therefore, the second issue brought about by temporal visions around media is one of *causality* and *determinism*: for instance, the democratisation of video game development is allegedly happening because of open-access game-production tools such as Twine, Unity and the Unreal Engine. Software that was once only accessible to large production studios is now easily downloadable from the Internet and released for free. Likewise, the new video game culture is supposedly being determined by the emergence of new categories of consumers.

Moreover, teleological narratives of technological progression produce the *freezing* of both present conditions and previous ones. Kember and Zylinska effectively summarise how linear narratives of technological progress are entangled with a deterministic view of media, one that freezes media into isolated tools. They also argue that such a process of isolation concerns the temporality of a 'developmental narrative':

The old versus new division . . . not only brings together affect and matter but also inscribes media into a progressive developmental narrative. In other words, it introduces the question of time into debates on media while simultaneously freezing this question by immediately dividing 'media time' into a series of discrete spatialized objects, or products that succeed one another. Thus we are said to progress from photography to Flickr, from books to e-readers.

Kember and Zylinska (2012, 3)

The narrative of progression – from what Sony had named the 1.0 era of gaming to the 2.0 and eventually 3.0 – can also be seen as establishing those ages and at the same time necessarily freezing the current scenario (Gaming 3.0) in an isolated space in the proposed linearity of technological development. What is more, these are rather predictable narratives: we can expect that the technical specifications and features of the next generation of video game consoles will increase exponentially from those of previous consoles. While describing the future of video games, these narratives simultaneously stop it in the present.

Creative Game Studies offers an alternative to the repetitive nature of the narratives surrounding video games and their players. First, Creative Game Studies aims at enabling an *intuitive* perspective, by giving things a new life, as Tim Ingold puts it (Ingold 2011). As I wrote at the beginning of this chapter, the video game industry is experiencing an identity crisis. The aim of Creative Game Studies is not to resolve the crisis but to state it through different words, thus inventing new problems that form a part of the crisis itself. Stating and inventing problems, rather than solving them, is precisely how Deleuze defines intuition, in his reading of Bergson (Deleuze 1988, 13–35). Inventing problems *intuitively* means recognising the existence of other durations, and seeing not just how things differ from each other in space, but also how they become different in time. Intuition introduces duration and movement into our accounts of the world surrounding us. Creative Game Studies investigates the processes of formation and transformation of things and time; it makes new cuts, and invents new forms of games and modes of being involved with them, thus avoiding the repetitiveness and predictability of the accounts that consider words and matter to be frozen in time. As a mode of intervention in video game culture, Creative Game Studies does not look at objects and time as finished and fragmented, but joins in their process of formation.

Creative Game Studies is aware of the duration and timing of the intervention. For an intervention to be *timely* it must participate in the surrounding environment and in the duration of things as they mutate and happen. In Chapter 3 I will look more specifically at the hacking of PlayStation Network. The boundaries of the console and online service offered by Sony have been mutating not just physically but also in time, and qualitatively, as their definitions were determined and contested by institutionalised actors participating in the trials that involved Sony. A creative reading of the hacking of PlayStation Network brings a destabilising view of this story, as a never-ending process of remediation in which the observer is involved (Bolter and Grusin 1999; Latour 2005; Michael 2000). It also demands that attention is paid to the timing of the enunciations provided by the actors involved (Sony, the hackers, and many others), and a consideration of when (years later) and with what effects my intervention takes place.

Creative Game Studies forces us to think of scholarly interventions as *performative*, as immersed and participating in the things they talk and write about. As I write about video game culture I become part of it, and I consider myself responsible for what I bring about. A creative reading is always and necessarily implicated in, and constitutive of, the narratives it creates. I believe that the intuitive invention of new problems is a form of fabulation; it makes new worlds replete with possibilities and impossibilities (Haraway 2011). This is evident in many of the aforementioned examples, where statements and public announcements by actors involved in the video game industry have effectively determined financial investments and the development of new products. However, performativity is also 'an empowering concept . . . because it not only explains how norms take place but also shows that change and invention are always possible' (Kember and Zylinska 2012, 189). Creative Game Studies takes the risk of being performative, potentially even in the sense of being theatrical: the on-stage announcements of expos such as E3, as much as the showmanship of TED Talk speakers, do not just present facts about the game industry, they also take full advantage of the fabulatory function of language. Creative Game Studies should not only try to produce a creative storytelling, but acknowledge that theory is also a performance (even when it presents itself as a mere description of reality).

However, Creative Game Studies should be able to tell the difference between the marketing talk of the TED series and critical intervention. A participative theory, in turn, involves the responsibility of having to make choices and pose questions that are going to be part of the discursive formation in which it intervenes. A creative study of games that takes into account its own performative potential must also necessarily be *ethical*, as criticality requires judgement and evaluation. The ethical question that I intend to pose, and not necessarily resolve, throughout the rest of this book concerns precisely the position of the researcher in the process of forming knowledge: what are the implications of avoiding essentialist and hegemonic approaches, and of attempting instead to multiply particularisms and differences through the invention of alternative narratives?

Moreover, the presentations of orderly successions of game products rarely consider the ideologies of progress associated with them, while taking the timely progression of technology as a given and as narrated by neutral voices. Thus, Creative Game Studies must also be *anti-authoritarian*, insofar as it must question the ways in which fossilised interpretations of the dynamics that compose video game culture are presented. Rather than replicating distinctions such as producer and consumer, independent and mainstream, or terms such as ownership, democratisation and freedom, Creative Game Studies will inquire into how such expressions have been framed, how they came into being, and how they could be otherwise. Following Michel Foucault and his inquiry into the construction of knowledge, Creative Game Studies poses the question of how power creates the conditions for making divisions, narrating the past, predicting the future, and more generally saying the truth (Foucault 1970, 1972, 1978,

1980). Creative Game Studies should produce anti-authoritarian narratives around video game culture, and these narratives should be produced as events of game culture, as timely intuitions that question the other co-existent stories around the medium.

Last but not least, Creative Game Studies is necessarily going to generate *anxiety* for the researcher. Thinking of video games as things that mutate in time, in which players and scholars are implicated as they look at and play with them, rather than as identifiable and finished products, can seem like an unstable foundation from which it is impossible to speak. However, academic scholarship has the imperative of 'making a cut', at one point, in these ongoing processes of mediation (Kember and Zylinska 2012). But how can significant cuts be made in this fluid scenario? To borrow the question posed by Ralph Waldo Emerson, quoted by Richard Grusin, it should be asked 'where do we find ourselves' if not at any of the extremes but always and necessarily in the connection itself, in mediation? (Grusin 2015).

Jacques Derrida expressed a similar feeling of insecurity while describing his own theory of deconstruction (Derrida 1976, 1980). Derrida observes how language creates meaning through structures of opposition between signs. Deconstruction is the process of reading and overturning oppositions in a text, and showing how meaning is always deferred, never present. The constant postponement of meaning introduces instability and uncertainty into language, and with this comes a potential sense of anxiety. Ultimately, in this book I turn to Derrida's understanding of anxiety to reveal the path to a creative study of gaming. Deconstruction offers to abandon the comfortable presence of existing categories and the theoretical possibilities resulting from them. Derrida argues that while anxiety is likely a necessary consequence of deconstruction, it is also a sign of being fully (one could say, ethically) involved in the 'game':

The concept of centered structure is in fact the concept of a freeplay based on a fundamental ground, a freeplay which is constituted upon a fundamental immobility and a reassuring certitude, which is itself beyond the reach of the freeplay. With this certitude anxiety can be mastered, for anxiety is invariably the result of a certain mode of being implicated in the game, of being caught by the game, of being as it were from the very beginning at stake in the game.

Derrida (1980, 248)

Creative Game Studies seeks to re-evaluate the possibility of being at play, within a study of gaming which becomes itself a form of play. This way of looking at things plays with given unities of discourse and aims to deconstruct the similarities and differences between groupings. The anxiety implied in this perspective results from acknowledging that there are always differences between the things that are usually kept together, and similarities between those things that are kept apart. The creative cut, the process of invention, consists in imagining those similarities and differences that are rarely, if ever, brought about.

Finally, what is Creative Game Studies? Creative Game Studies is just like a new video game. It is a video game available on Mac and PC, to be played on pre-installed text-editing software. It is the digital version of a previous pen-and-paper game. The game is played by writing words about video games, words that are constitutive of the medium itself. In this book I offer the results of a prolonged session of mine with this new video game. Creative Game Studies proposes to be an *intuitive, timely, performative, ethical, anti-authoritarian* and *anxious* way of writing about video games. Paraphrasing J. L. Austin, Creative Game Studies poses the question of how to do things with Microsoft Word: how to intervene in video game culture by writing about it (Austin 1962).

What Is in This Book?

Throughout this book I will propose different readings of recent events and stories that surround contemporary video game culture. Some of these stories will be very personal. In the first chapter, I reflect on my experience with the Nike+ FuelBand wristband, a device used to count the daily steps and monitor the physical activity of the user. Experts have described Nike+ FuelBand as an example of the larger trend of gamification, or the 'use of game design elements in non-game contexts' (Deterding et al. 2011). Allegedly, gamification aims at creating a deep 'engagement' with the user, in order not just to quantify their practices but also to influence their behaviour (Zichermann and Cunningham 2011). However, after two years of wearing Nike+ FuelBand, and having spent so much time in physical contact with it, I started to feel that my engagement was becoming more like that of a couple in a romantic relationship. The future moment of radical modification of my behaviour seemed to be continuously postponed, and it mostly consisted of boring, repetitive activities. In the chapter, I reflect on my own decision to break the relationship: a hard decision to take, particularly when the basic principles of gamification eliminate the possibility of any event or rupture, proposing instead a homogeneous understanding of time and space. In such conditions, it was not easy to find a good excuse to justify the break-up.

Eventually, I managed to stop wearing Nike+ FuelBand. In my life after gamification, I started playing again with my unquantified self. Ultimately, in the chapter I propose the possibility of reimagining the notion of engagement with games and technologies, and the very idea that both players and games could act and have an influence on each other. Instead I introduce other modes for thinking about our relationships: as processes of dwelling in gamified technologies, and in terms of kinship (Heidegger 1971a; Ingold 2011; Haraway 2004, 2015). At stake is the possibility of imagining a more lively engagement with our gamified selves – an engagement that brings partial, strategic and temporary knowledge about ourselves and the games we live with.

While looking at alternative forms of engagement with video games, I explored the stories of developers who decided to work independently by making and releasing their own digital products. The field of independent production, which has attracted many who worked in the industry in the last decade, has opened the way to new forms of management of the development process. It is now relatively common for an individual or a small group to work on a video game independently, thanks to freely available development software. The meaning of independence, in this context, is disputed. Does it mean that the developer works in opposition to the mainstream industry? Does it involve the choice of tools used for programming the game? Or does it affect the content and aesthetic of the product itself? Is it a political choice, a business model, or mostly a style of game design?

Indeed, the answer is not straightforward and differs from case to case. In Chapter 2, I argue that independence is a concept that forces the individual developers to talk about and define themselves in terms of their own independence and of what they intend to do with their games. Thus, it offers an original ethical question: independent developers discuss, during the many occasions on which they are asked to describe their own practice, their own presence in the world, and in relation to the others (be they other independents or the game industry). The creation of otherness is necessary in the development of the independent individual, but neither the individual nor its outside (the otherness needed to differentiate oneself) can ever be fully grasped. As a floating signifier, independence is productive precisely because of its unresolvable condition (Laclau 1996). The notion of independence produces unstable and constantly negotiated boundaries between oneself and others. Indeed, there are many different ways to structure this discourse of self-definition. Incubators and workshops for independent developers ultimately offer a way of planning one's own career by knowing and taking care of the self (Foucault 1998). Other negotiations of the concept are open to forms of self-ghettoisation, narcissism and solipsism. Ultimately, the ethical question of independence transforms the relation between the developer and their game into a pressing one that needs to be continually discussed. At stake is the possibility of imagining new forms of hospitality within the culture of video game development, by interpreting independence as an ethical question of how best to relate to the other-which-is-not-me (Zerilli 2006).

While independent developers define and construct themselves as independents, video game products are similarly subject to processes of negotiation and redefinition. In Chapters 3 and 4, I explore two events of game culture, quite distinct but each placing at the centre a question of what a video game could become, and of what it is. In Chapter 3, I look at the hacking of PlayStation Network. Sony's console and its online service have been hacked numerous times since March 2011, when Sony decided to remove a feature of the PlayStation 3 console that could have been exploited for acts of digital piracy. Many consumers saw this decision as authoritarian and dishonest, as they had bought a console which was later altered by its producer. The series of events following on from that moment have provoked conflicting ideas about who owns a video game console, and who has the right and freedom to manipulate it. Ultimately, the question became one of ontology: what is PlayStation Network?

In the chapter, I expand the problem, rather than resolving it, by looking at how Sony's attorney at the California State Court came up with a solution while defending the video game publisher. She pointed at the product's warranty, which claims that Sony cannot be responsible for any malfunctioning after one year from the date of purchase. Thus, Sony could not be held responsible for having changed a single feature of a product, which could stop functioning completely with no legal repercussions for its publisher. However, by introducing the notion of time into the definition of what constitutes a video game console, she suggested that definitions of digital products are temporary: these definitions are strategic, have their own timing (given that the authorities and locations associated with these utterances matter), and inscribe technologies in time, deciding what they are before and after the act of definition.

In the chapter, I intervene creatively and critically in PlayStation Network by questioning how and by whom the boundaries of the network are drawn, how the network changes in time, and how long it takes to change it again. I explore the role of the hacker, the actor who modifies the PlayStation Network and transforms its boundaries and physical limits in the process. The hacker can be seen as a hybrid mediator who is involved in the same network he or she modifies (Latour 2005, Michael 2000). Being part of the network itself, the hacker can be reinterpreted as a much broader figure, one that includes Sony's attorney, for instance, and myself, author of this chapter, as further mediators of the story of the hacking of PlayStation Network, in addition to everyone who plays with the console and alters its shape by manipulating it physically, intellectually and intuitively. In the end, looking at the presence and interventions of hackers in the network of material and immaterial nodes that make a video game console, one sees how consoles leak not just when their databases are illegitimately accessed, but *all the time*: consoles are malleable and modified continuously; they are comprised of tangible and intangible nodes that, in time, change their state of matter and their relations with each other.

In Chapter 4, I look at another event that destabilised the boundaries of what is conceived to be a video game. The story of *E.T. the Extra-Terrestrial*, a video game inspired by the Steven Spielberg movie, has its roots in Atari's economic failure during the crash of the video game industry between 1982 and 1985. When Atari published the game, the sales were so disappointing that Atari could not afford to store all the unsold cartridges. As urban legend has it, Atari decided to dump these cartridges in the desert of New Mexico. After around 30 years, a movie company decided to shoot a documentary about this story and dig in the desert in search of proof of the existence of *E.T.* What they found turned out to be much more destabilising and unsettling than they could have hoped for.

The story of *E.T.* and its 'afterlife' offers an example of how the telling of a medium's past can work to reinforce its own present and, effectively, write its future. The archaeological perspective adopts the metaphor of the physical excavation – a metaphor which became literal in the case of *E.T.* (Huhtamo and Parikka 2011; Parikka 2012; Guins 2014; Suominen 2016). However, the act of digging in the mud to discover the past events of a medium's history stabilises the present by assuming it as a safe telos of historical developments. In particular, the story of *E.T.* reveals a certain obsession with thinking of video games as boxes, as tangible pieces of plastic and silicon. Even when looking at the disputed issue of the first ever video game, as I discuss in the chapter, the historiographies serve to reduce early computer experiments to identifiable unities. Thus, the history of video games is looked at as the history of its products and consumers, and stories such as that of *E.T.* appear to us as stories of a failed product, as exceptions that merely confirm the homogeneous progression towards what the medium is today. My intervention in the story of *E.T.* consists in writing a history of the present, as intended in the genealogical project by Michel Foucault (Foucault 1970, 1972, 1991). In this view, the present itself becomes a unity of discourse caught while in its undoing. The apparent unity of *E.T. the Extra-Terrestrial* is in fact revealed to be as porous and fragile as Sony's PlayStation Network: as soon as it was recovered from the mud, it became an unstable object, bringing gamers and journalists to anxiously question the conditions of possibility for talking about the past, present and future of a medium.

In Chapter 5, I discuss another series of recent events that have prompted a reinterpretation of the history and future of the medium from a different standpoint than that of the video game archaeologists of *E.T.* The GamerGate controversy has been marked by a series of misogynist attacks perpetrated by male gamers who were concerned about the presence of women in video game culture. The campaign started after game designer Zoe Quinn was accused of having a conflict of interest with a journalist from the online magazine *Kotaku*. The campaign quickly degenerated and targeted many of the women who took a stand in support of Quinn, until it even included academia and the Digital Games Research Association as part of a supposed feminist plot to take over the game industry. The plot was allegedly aimed at controlling the medium by imposing gender equality. On the other side, GamerGate supporters felt entitled to decide how the medium should be, defining themselves as the true, passionate gamers who originally constituted the majority of consumers. GamerGate still generates tweets and posts on Reddit and 4chan, and at its peak, between 2014 and 2015, some of the targeted women received death threats and personal accusations at their private addresses.

In this story of hate and misogynistic campaigns, in all the conspiratorial narratives that were used to accuse women who create and write about games, where do I find myself? What can be said, and what is the value of speaking, when the number of comments and stories is so abundant that any opinion seems equally irrelevant? In the chapter, I start from one comment left on Reddit by one of the thousands of users who supported GamerGate. In the comment, the user accused academia of being like a parasite that does not produce anything. In respect to GamerGate, this is a particularly appropriate comment: it is almost impossible to have an influence on a debate that has generated innumerable contradictory and conspiratorial narratives. However, the idea of being parasitical might prove to be a useful metaphor.

In the chapter I turn to the parasite as a figure to understand my role and presence within the stories of video game culture (Serres 1982). A parasite, in the work of Serres, is understood as something living in symbiotic relation with another organism. The parasite is an exploiter, but at the same time it destabilises the boundaries of a system by living at its margins. The parasite is neither inside nor outside, neither part of the organism it exploits nor independent from it. In relation to GamerGate, thinking of myself as a parasite means avoiding the binarism of being inside or outside game culture, and as a parasite I can look at the history of games not in terms of the categories of people who allegedly step in or out of it, but as something anyone can always relate to and rewrite. Being a parasite is not necessarily a negative condition, as Serres argues. In fact, parasites occasionally bring vital modifications to the exploited organisms, giving them new life (in biology, this would be defined as a symbiotic relationship).

I look at some examples, such as the stories of Roberta Williams and Anna Anthropy, of women who have been approaching digital games as parasites of the good kind by designing, talking and thinking about video games (Nooney 2013; Anthropy 2012). In these circumstances, video game culture has been rewritten from strategic vantage points, introducing alternative histories, uses and modes of production. Intervening in game culture as parasites is another way of thinking and acting creatively, as can be learnt by looking at some of the responses given to GamerGate and its campaigns of harassment.

In the conclusion, I try to answer one final question: what is the value of writing about video games? What is at stake in Creative Game Studies, in this new video game that I have been trying to play while writing this book? A new product, released while finalising this manuscript, offers a possible answer. The game *Pokémon Go*, by Niantic, an instant success on the Apple and Google digital stores, reminds its players at the outset to be 'alert at all times [and] stay aware of your surroundings'. By way of conclusion, I note that Creative Game Studies consists of this: it is a self-imposed pressure to be alert *to* all times and timings, those of the narratives of the future produced by the industry, but also the time needed to write about the medium of the video game. Creative Game Studies invites us to think of these different timings as possibilities for alternative creative interventions within video game culture and, ultimately, to imagine different ways of being involved 'in our surroundings'.

1

···

Life after Gamification: How I Broke Up with Nike+ FuelBand

I decided to break up with Nike+ FuelBand after wearing the wristband for more than two years. After an initial period of enthusiasm, I realised that I was no longer sure whether I really wanted to continue using Nike's gadget. The problem I had with Nike+ FuelBand was not specifically related to the product itself but to the broader concept of *gamification*, a trend in the design of digital products that has directly inspired the development of Nike's gadget. Gamification, broadly defined as the application of game design techniques in non-playful contexts, has been interpreted by several marketing and design gurus as the future in the use of digital technologies for civic and social engagement (Deterding et al. 2011; McGonigal 2011; Fuchs et al. 2014). In this chapter, I would like to analyse my own relationship with Nike+ FuelBand, looking at how it started and then came to an end, and how this personal story might have repercussions for the notion of gamification. This will be a way for me to reflect on what I have done, and what I want to be: after two years of an intense relationship with Nike+ FuelBand, I feel like it is now time to take care of my (unquantified) self.

Nike+ FuelBand is often presented as an example of larger trends in the production of technologies for the control and improvement of the body through game-like scenarios. Nike+ FuelBand uses the NikeFuel unit of measurement produced by the sports company Nike. It is sold as a wristband to be worn by the user during the day and while carrying out any activity. While the gadget is worn, an accelerometer inserted in the wristband converts the movement of the body into a score. The score is visible from the wristband itself, by pressing a button, or by connecting the gadget to a laptop or smartphone via Bluetooth. At midnight the score resets and the counting starts again from zero. Nike+ FuelBand is designed for sport practitioners as well as beginners, and it is advertised as a tool for self-improvement by self-tracking.

According to experts, Nike+ FuelBand exemplifies the phenomenon of gamification. Gamification is a current trend in the design of apps and services for self-improvement (through health, education and learning), and for attracting customers to new or existing businesses. According to Deterding et al., gamification is the practice of introducing game design elements into contexts that otherwise would not be defined as games. Game design elements are broadly intended as 'elements that are *characteristic to* games' (Deterding et al. 2011, 3). More specifically, these are usually interface and game design patterns such as badges, levels, scores, rankings, leaderboards and rewards.

Mathias Fuchs looks at gamification as part of a larger trend within modernity, one that makes use of quantification practices in diverse spheres of social life such as religion and the economy (Fuchs 2014). Joost Raessens thinks of gamification as part of the broader phenomenon of ludification, or the 'ludic turn': the permeation of playful elements into real life and 'serious' experiences, a trend which is becoming more and more pervasive in contemporary culture (Raessens 2014). Extensive use of the term has been reported since 2010, while its origins are probably to be found in a consultancy company, Conundra, founded in 2003 by game designer Nick Pelling, who claimed to be specialising in gamification (Deterding et al. 2011; Werbach and Hunter 2012). Conundra focused on offering consultancies to companies interested in attracting new customers by implementing game features in their offer. In more recent times, the idea of gamifying a business has re-emerged, not necessarily with direct reference to Pelling's first attempt but similarly presented as a technique to be sold to companies via consultancies.

Since 2011, the marketing/consultancy sector has been re-evaluating gamification as a potential source of revenue. The last few years have also witnessed the emergence of several events and publications that have contributed to defining gamification. Gabe Zichermann and Christopher Cunningham's text *Gamification by Design: Implementing Game Mechanics in Web and Mobile Apps* is the most popular, as are Zichermann's website Gamification.co and the associated annual conference, Gamification Summit, held in San Francisco every year since 2011 (Zichermann and Cunningham 2011). Jane McGonigal's work, culminating in her contribution at the TED Talk series in 2010, is also concerned with selling gamification to corporations. Jane McGonigal's talk at TED 'Gaming Can Make a Better World' has been viewed by more than 4 million people since its publication, according to the TED website (McGonigal 2010). In McGonigal's view, gamification (although she does not use the term explicitly) is a new goldmine for designers and business makers. It is also a tool for social policy and, more broadly, for changing and 'healing' the world (BBC 2016).

Gamification appears to group together a number of very different practices. On Gamification.co, the main online reference for finding out about new experiments and products in the field, gamification is applied to a range of different areas. At the time of writing, the website appears to be no longer updated, but just by looking at one week's worth of news we can see that gamification can improve the learning of mathematics in schools ('Facilitating Math Learning with DreamBox Learning Platform', 1 March 2016), brand loyalty and customer retention ('CataBoom: Sparking Brand Loyalty with Rewarding Games', 29 February 2016), work environments and employees' health ('Welltok Gamifies Employee's Journey to Wellness', 24 February 2016), and sexual health ('Gamifying Sexual Health with OhMiBod's Lovelife Krush', 23 February 2016). Other oft-cited examples are the Miles Club's offers from airline companies, where customers receive bonuses by buying numerous flights with the same company, and coffee shops offering free drinks after a certain number of purchases at the same chain (Zichermann and Cunningham 2011; Schrape 2014).

Textbooks on the subject present gamification as a technique based on the collection and analysis of previous experiences in user engagement (Zichermann and Cunningham 2011). Gamification is thereby presented as a series of practical and operational suggestions about how to involve users (be they customers, citizens, employees or gamers) and how to maximise their performance towards a specific goal. In order to achieve such an ambitious goal, gamified technologies must collect and archive user data. Data first needs to be archived and processed to later become part of a game; it is collected according to a principle of transparency: gamification plays with the facts about the user and attempts to assist the user in enhancing these same facts, these truths about him- or herself.

This very notion of the self is evoked by the Quantified Self movement. The origins of the Quantified Self movement are somewhat similar to those in which gamification was first promoted. In a TED Talk series, around 2010, the idea of the Quantified Self received major exposure through the words of experts involved, mostly, in the editorial team of *Wired* magazine.[1] The movement promotes the introduction of technologies for the measurement of daily activities in individuals' lives. Collection and data processing is oriented towards the improvement of life, here intended as the sum of the data about a person's body as it is generated during daily activities. The Quantified Self is also promoted as a solution to medical problems and for the improvement of certain bodily characteristics. Gamification can actually be seen as a further step in the process of quantifying the self, in which the improvement of life happens through a game-like environment, and in establishing practices of participation between users.

The Meaning of Engagement

One of the keywords within the discourses surrounding gamification is *engagement*. Many authors see engagement as the Holy Grail of gamification, as it is used to discuss and represent the extent to which players are using the game and being influenced by it. Zichermann and Cunningham begin their text with a definition of engagement:

The term 'engagement', in a business sense, indicates the connection between a consumer and a product or service. Unsurprisingly, the term is also used to name the period in a romantic couple's relationship during which they are preparing and planning to spend the rest of their lives together. Engagement is the period of time at which we have a great deal of connection with a person, place, thing or idea.

(2011, xvi)

---

[1] Gary Wolf, author and contributing editor at *Wired* magazine, presented his idea of the quantified self at a TED Talk in June 2010 (www.ted.com/talks/gary_wolf_the_quantified_self, accessed 29 January 2017) and during the *Wired* Health Conference: Living by Numbers, October 2012 (www.wired.com/2012/10/wired-health-conference/). Gary Wolf has often presented Nike+ FuelBand as an example of the Quantified Self.

However, for Zichermann and Cunningham, this definition is a problem because it is too broad. Therefore they propose to create a metric to break down engagement:

We would be better off thinking of engagement as being comprised of a series of potentially interrelated metrics that combine to form a whole. These metrics are: recency, frequency, duration, virality, ratings. Collectively, they can be amalgamated as an 'E' (or engagement) score.

(2011, xvi)

Rather than taking this prosaic definition, I prefer to think through the metaphor of engagement in the broadest possible way, perhaps even taking to its logical conclusion the romantic interpretation that Zichermann and Cunningham so quickly dismissed. After all, my own engagement with Nike+ FuelBand lasted for such a long time that it is difficult now to evaluate the 'E' score of our relationship. Our engagement looked much more like that of a couple in a romantic relationship and, after two years, we could easily have spent the rest of our lives together. The relationship we had was very intimate. Nike+ FuelBand was always on my wrist, and I would always take it with me. Nike+ FuelBand knew a lot about me, but it also needed my movement to increase the score on the wristband, and I had to regularly recharge it to maintain its functionality. Nike+ FuelBand was completely dependent on my presence and care. I would check my score more than once a day, while it was closely attached to my wrist. We were always touching each other.

Engagement is a special kind of relationship, one that precedes the passage towards a more binding relationship. It is a kind of relationship that is expected to change drastically at one point and transform itself into something different. A romantic engagement is supposed to change on the day of the wedding. In mathematics, sudden changes that alter a status of quiet and which result from minor alterations are defined as catastrophes. Although not everyone would agree that a wedding is a catastrophic event, it certainly has the characteristics of a catastrophe in the mathematical sense: it is an event which radically changes the relationship between a couple, in a way that cannot be undone – it can of course be altered again if a separation, or a divorce, occurs, but this again would be a catastrophic event.

Thus, engagement is, by definition, expected to end at one point and transform into something else. Engagement implies change and *movement* towards a catastrophic point of modification, or progress towards an event that will alter the terms of the engagement itself. Engagement makes sense only in its duration, in its mutations in time.

A Static Conception of Movement

Movement, as a matter of fact, is the most important keyword in the marketing of Nike+ FuelBand. It is advertised as a technology for the measurement of movement, and Nike understands movement as equivalent to life. When I decided to buy Nike+ FuelBand and keep it on my wrist all the time, I was attracted by the bold statement in the advertisement. A video published by the sports company in 2013 explains what the gadget is about:

Our minds, our bodies and our experience all tell us that movement is life and that the more we move the more we live. It's something athletes have understood from the beginning. The kind of movement it takes to improve your game is the kind of movement it takes to improve your life. But unlike sport, life doesn't come with convenient ways of measuring movement. So we developed one. Nike+ FuelBand: a single universal unit uniquely designed to measure the movement of the entire human body for the entire human race, whatever your weight, whatever your gender, whatever your activity. It's that simple and that revolutionary. So get out there, find what fuels you and get moving.

This Is Nike+ FuelBand (2013)

The video shows people of different ages and races practising sports, at more or less professional levels. They all move; therefore, they all live, according to the syllogism implicit in the advertisement.

Indeed, the problem of quantifying movement is one of the oldest in Western philosophy, and Nike's product, from this point of view, certainly stands on the shoulders of giants. The philosophical question posed by the paradox of Zeno of Elea, in the fifth century BC, could find a major contribution in the form of Nike+ FuelBand. In this paradox, Zeno imagines that Achilles, one of the main characters in Greek mythology and a notoriously fast runner, engages in a race with a tortoise. To compensate for its disadvantage, the tortoise is given a head start over Achilles. When the race begins, each contestant will run at a constant speed, but while Achilles will move at a fast pace, the tortoise will proceed very slowly. Common sense suggests that Achilles will quickly outrun the tortoise. Instead, according to Zeno, Achilles will never reach the animal. In fact, Zeno argues, Achilles must first cover half the distance that separates himself from the tortoise, and before running half the distance, he has to cover a quarter of the distance, and so on. While he does so, the tortoise also proceeds further. The gap between the two will never be covered because it can be divided an infinite number of times, thus making the task of reaching the tortoise an infinite and impossible task for Achilles.

Henri Bergson challenged the paradox in his *Time and Free Will: An Essay on the Immediate Data of Consciousness* (Bergson 2001). In Bergson's view, Achilles will certainly reach and pass the tortoise. However, the example formulated by Zeno will remain unsolvable as long as movement is spatialised, as Bergson puts it. Intuition tells us that Achilles will run faster than the tortoise because movement has its own duration, and duration cannot be reduced to space. The space surrounding Achilles and the tortoise is homogeneous and can be divided into infinitely smaller fragments. However, the movements of Achilles and the tortoise are not similarly homogeneous and happen in time as much as in space. Movements are indivisible and different *in kind* in respect to the space occupied by Achilles and the tortoise:

Why does Achilles outstrip the tortoise? Because each of Achilles' steps and each of the tortoise's steps are indivisible acts in so far as they are movements, and are different magnitudes in so far as they are space . . . This is what Zeno leaves out of account when he reconstructs the movement of Achilles . . . forgetting that space alone can be divided and put together again in any way we like, and thus confusing space with motion.

Bergson (2001, 113–14)

Bergson solves the paradox through what he calls 'intuition', that is '[stating] a problem and [solving] it in terms of time rather than of space' (Deleuze 1988, 31). The sports company Nike instead reinforces the paradox by spatialising movement (and life with it). Bergson would say that Nike makes use of intellect rather than intuition. The two terms are crucial in Bergson's philosophy. While intellect is analytical, in that it divides and recomposes things in order to give us the knowledge we need to satisfy our needs, intuition instead gives us the knowledge of how things are in constant movement and always in the process of becoming other (Bergson 2007). Intellectual approaches to reality understand it pragmatically, analytically and quantitatively. Intelligence makes human beings look at things in their homogeneity, so that they can be counted and quantified. Bergson presents the example of a flock of sheep, which can be seen as a homogeneous group, but each sheep can be spatially separated from the other and enumerated – this is what Bergson calls a quantitative multiplicity (2001, 76–77). Intuition offers a different capacity to our minds, one that reconnects us with the vital impulse (*élan vital*) shared by all living species. Through intuition we understand duration, continuity and change. Bergson offers the example of the feeling of sympathy towards another human being. The feeling changes qualitatively in time but without ever making it possible for us to spatially separate the different kinds of sympathy that we have been experiencing through time (2001, 18–19).

Space is homogeneous, but movement is not. Movement is an event that has its own duration, as it happens in time as much as in space. However, Nike understands movement and space in a way that reinforces the paradox of Zeno. The movement of the user must be recorded through an accelerometer and transformed into a score which can increase in quantity, but where every unit is qualitatively the same as any other unit: the movement needed to move from zero to one NikeFuel-point is supposedly of the same intensity and quality as that which is required to increase the score from one to two. Thus, in Nike+ FuelBand, movement is spatialised as it is represented as a continuum of homogeneous units. If Achilles and the tortoise were given a Nike wristband, Zeno could have divided their scores into infinitely smaller portions to prove his argument.

Thus, Nike understands movement as something rather static, and I am afraid that such a static movement has been a major problem in my engagement with Nike+ FuelBand.

A Technical Fault

In fact, during our two years of engagement, one event occurred which changed the relationship between myself and Nike+ FuelBand. It did not raise any particular concern at the time, but it later gave me good reason to rethink the value of our engagement. About nine months from the date of purchase, the wristband was not working properly. My scores were retrospectively changed when I connected the app on my smartphone, thus making the records unusable for comparisons. I wrote to Nike's account on Twitter (@NikeSupport) for several weeks, but despite their generous assistance, I had to claim a replacement and collect a new wristband at the Nike Store in Oxford Circus, London. The new Nike+ FuelBand worked exactly like the previous one, and at first I did not consider this passage to be in any way significant to our engagement.

However, one year later I started questioning that moment in our relationship when the wristband was replaced. Was I engaging with the wristband I had once replaced, or with the new one? Or was I supposed to engage with NikeFuel as an abstract concept, with the score itself, regardless of the device on my wrist? Most importantly, and tragically: what if something happened to me? What if I stopped moving (or living)? Could my Nike+ FuelBand wristband replace me with someone else? If a different person picked up and wore the product, it would continue working in the same way as it did with me. In this relationship each of us was replaceable.

Relationships often come to an end when an unexpected event (the start of another affair, moving town, changing job, and so on) occurs, a rupture in an established order which makes the previous condition impossible to recover. Catastrophes of this kind cannot be undone. In those circumstances, it is usually said that nothing can ever be the same again. In my case, instead, I started to realise that by swapping the wristband with a new one, everything would always stay the same, forever. This is, unfortunately, far more dramatic.

In Zeno's paradox, the two main actors – Achilles and the tortoise – can be replaced. The choice of these two characters works well in the narrative of the paradox because one represents a fast-running mythological hero, while the other is a slow-moving animal. However, the paradox becomes relevant because it is not just a personal problem of Achilles, or of the tortoise; it also concerns the conception of movement in general, at any time and in any place. In Zeno's paradox, Achilles will never outrun the tortoise, but also, in the view of the Greek philosopher, nor could anyone else in any other context, at any given time.

Zeno's paradox applies to any possible race or movement performed by anyone, at any time and at any latitude or longitude of the globe. Similarly, the NikeFuel score matters to its user because it will be used to compare any future performance, and this is possible because the gadget will work in the same way at any given time and place. Nike says this explicitly in its advertisement: Nike+ FuelBand is supposed to 'measure the movement of the entire human body for the entire human race, whatever your weight, whatever your gender, whatever your activity' (This Is Nike+ FuelBand 2013). Nike will measure the user's movement, whoever and wherever the user is or will be. For the gadget to have any value, it must not just record the movement happening at the present time but also any other movements in the future. Time and space, after all, have a homogeneous quality in Nike's interpretation.

After these considerations, I reached the conclusion that Nike+ FuelBand and I could replace one another with no significant consequences. In other words, the daily scores accumulated over two years, while distinct in their degree or intensity, were unlikely to ever become of a different *kind*, that is, of a different quality, one that would be incomparable and indivisible by the same criteria applied to all the other previous and future movements. Gamification aims at a kind of engagement which ultimately remains static, rather than being dynamic. Taking Nike+ FuelBand as an example, it is clear how the very tension towards the future is crystallised. The game never ends, and the next day's engagement will be measured and evaluated through the same criteria as that of the present day. If this were a romantic engagement, it could be said that Nike+ FuelBand is a wristband that never becomes a wedding ring.

Could the relationship be changed? Could I play differently with Nike+ FuelBand, and gamification in general? Could our engagement be somehow transformed into something different? Nike+ FuelBand cannot be easily hacked or modified into anything other than what it is at the time of purchase. The only choice left to the user consists in either wearing the wristband or not wearing it. However, I believe that engagement with gamified apps can be rethought by reconsidering the distance between the gadgets or apps that are supposed to quantify users' lives on the one hand, and their bodies, minds, movements and intuitions on the other. The problem with engagement in gamification (and the same could be said of the broader Quantified Self movement) is that it implies a certain commitment and mutual influence between user and technology, while keeping both at a distance. Such distance never really changes or develops into a different kind of intimacy. The influence exercised by the technology on the user and by the user on the technology, which texts on gamification define as engagement, can otherwise be defined as a problem with the unbridgeable distance that keeps user and technology separate and aloof from one another. This notion is often discussed in terms of *agency*.

The Problem with Agency

Many scholars, particularly from video game studies, have severely criticised gamification. Ian Bogost has been one of the most fervent critics. In May 2011, a post on Gamasutra written by Bogost defined gamification as 'exploitationware', as it replaces 'real incentives with fictional ones', and 'real, functional, two-way relationships with dysfunctional perversions of relationships. Organizations ask for loyalty, but they reciprocate that loyalty with shams, counterfeit incentives that neither provide value nor require investment' (Bogost 2011a). In August 2011, he illustrated his position further, claiming that 'gamification is bullshit', as it is used to 'conceal, impress or coerce' (Bogost 2015). While gamification seems to be just a keyword now used to embellish thefts and scams, Bogost argues that other possibilities are open for game design to have an impact in areas such as health, education and work management.

Bogost explored this perspective in *How to Do Things with Videogames*, which does not directly refer to gamification but could be read as a follow-up to the aforementioned articles (Bogost 2011b). Here the reference to Austin's *How to Do Things with Words* is explicit in the title, as is the attempt to spark a debate about the potential of video games from a perspective that is more nuanced than that surrounding gamification (Austin 1962). This means, according to Bogost, that a better understanding of the potential of digital games entails an expansion of the number of things attainable from them: to be used not only for entertainment or as part of marketing campaigns and self-help applications, as proposed in gamification, but also as objects with an artistic value or as elements of social and political campaigns, and much more. Just as

Austin thought of language, more broadly, to have a performative potential, that is, to make changes in the world it mentions and describes, so Bogost believes that games can do things, and engage the player in relatively controllable ways.

In *How to Do Things with Videogames*, Bogost makes a list of some of the possible uses of digital games as these have emerged in recent times, including games with political content, promotional games displaying in-game advertisements, games used for propaganda or activism, and those with artistic purposes. He also discusses, through several short chapters, how games could evoke 'empathy', 'reverence', 'relaxation', 'disinterest' and 'drill', among other affects. Bogost argues that the relevance of a medium can be understood by looking at the variety of things it does: 'we can think of a medium's explored uses as a spectrum, a possibility space that extends from purely artistic uses at one end . . . to purely instrumental uses at the other' (Bogost 2011b, 3).

Bogost's answer to the debates on the potential of the medium of the video game is to avoid binaries and oppositions between serious and superficial technologies. He proposes instead what he calls an ecological understanding of the medium, inspired by Marshall McLuhan and Neil Postman's theory of media (McLuhan 1964; Postman 1992). In this view, according to Bogost, media affect the environment into which they are introduced at a variety of levels, and these need not be evaluated in positive or negative terms. Bogost's response to gamification, and more broadly to the idea that video games can be used to achieve specific effects, challenges the institutionalisation and appropriation of the alleged transformations of the medium through gamification that come from the marketing side. However, it does little to uncover the origins of such views. More importantly, it does not yet complicate or possibly surpass the binaries he evokes, and therefore does not propose a way of thinking about video games that could be seen as radically different from what Jane McGonigal and Gabe Zichermann and his colleagues evangelise about. The question of what can be done with video games receives a more varied response from Bogost than from any of the gamification gurus. However, what persists is the idea that the medium of the video game has a certain impact on its users – an impact that could be more or less predicted and channelled through design.

The problem with this view can be summarised as a question of the role and value attributed to *agency*. The agency of technologies concerns the potential for action that these have on their users, and that users have on them. The problem with this notion is that it reduces the mutual effects between users and technologies (the engagement) to transitive and hypothetical flows that move from human bodies to the tools they use, and vice versa. The transitivity of agency is also reflected in the verbs usually chosen to discuss it: technologies are said to influence, affect, alter, cause, consume, produce, do something to each other. These are transitive verbs that imply movement, from subject to object, while keeping the two distant.

Agency, and the essentially transitive actions that it implies, has been questioned in the work of Martin Heidegger, who offered instead the concept of 'dwelling', in the essay 'Building Dwelling Thinking' (Heidegger 1971a). Dwelling, an intransitive verb, is not directed towards an object and should not be taken as a direct consequence, or as the opposite, of the act of building (for instance, as consumption could be seen in relation to production). Dwelling is rather a way of being which is understood as becoming rather than as something permanent. Dwelling in the environment means being present not as static points, standing in one place and separated from the things that are observed and used, but as deeply involved in the surrounding reality.

Tim Ingold explored the work of Heidegger further and put it in relation to the notion of agency (Ingold 2010, 2011). As Ingold argues, agency is a term often brought into a debate in order to resuscitate the concept of materiality. In this view, objects have a certain material presence that does something to those who are near them; they have agency with regard to the surrounding environment. However, Ingold suggests that thinking in this way tends to suffocate humans and objects by 'the dead hand of materiality' (Ingold 2011, 28): all that is material stands still, engages with the surrounding environment and is put in motion by a sort of 'magical mind-dust' (Ingold 2010, 2) that is agency. Agency and materiality are not only forms of abstraction that overshadow the nuanced relations between human beings and the surrounding environment, but, as concepts, they also actively produce this distinction.

The problem of agency is deeply entwined in the ideas of movement and quantification as embedded in discourses on gamification, as these notions tend to immobilise users and the tools surrounding them. Agency assumes an unbridgeable gap between human beings and the environment. The gap is what effectively prevents engagement with gamified apps from ever mutating in time and transforming into something different. To fill that gap, what is needed is an intuition of a different *kind* that could transform the engagement with gamification, and with games and technologies in general, into something radically different.

A Different Game: From Agency to Life

Thus, agency appears as the central, overlooked issue around which discourses of engagement with games and gamification are framed. The *things to do with* games imply that both players and games have a potential for action, a margin of influence and impact on each other.

My argument is that the problem of agency in relation to gamification has been understood so far in a rather rationalist manner, that is, through a perspective whereby 'the concatenation of causes and consequences . . . does not trigger any dramatic effect, because, precisely . . . the consequences are *already there* in the cause: no suspense to expect, no sudden transformation, no metamorphosis, no ambiguity. Time flows from *past to present*' (Latour 2014, 11). Nike+ FuelBand, for instance, is a system that is designed to receive and record already predicted signals; it rewards precise events that are already expected by the simulation. The runner/player of Nike+ FuelBand is encouraged to comply with a set of rules that works as a regulatory frame, where only specific events are expected, saved, calculated and evaluated. Through this practice of compliance, the user of Nike+ FuelBand is normalised and regulates him- or herself in order to maintain and progress in a process of constant self-normalisation and discipline (Foucault 1977; Whitson 2015).

Latour notes that agents have meaning because of their acting, which also means that 'for all agents, acting means having their existence, their subsistence, come *from the future to the present*' (2014, 13). In what he calls the 'scientific world view', by contrast, Latour argues that 'nothing happens any more since the agent is supposed to be "simply caused" by its predecessor' (2014, 14). What does this lack of events amount to? Agency becomes a rather strangling perspective of the surrounding world. Actors are seen as abstracted from the environment and acting on the nearby objects through a cause–effect relation, one in which temporality is linear, irreversible, and as spatialised and homogeneous as the actions that happen through it.

For Nike+ FuelBand to achieve a felicitous engagement with its user, it should be assumed that the two objects participating in the relationship (the user and the wristband) could influence each other by proximity. For this event to happen through the agency of the two participating actors, both sides need to be put in motion by a force which is neither easy to define nor simple to grasp intellectually.

To bypass the dead-end of agency, Ingold proposes that we rethink our relation to the environment. An essential step for doing this is to think less about objects and more about *things*. Ingold draws on Heidegger's essay 'The Thing' in arguing that the distinction between objects and things can be crucial when evaluating what is at stake in the debates around agency and, as I will argue, it could prove useful in evaluating gamification (Heidegger 1971b). Ingold comments:

> The object stands before us as a *fait accompli*, presenting its congealed, outer surfaces to our inspection. It is defined by its very 'overagainstness' in relation to the setting in which it is placed (Heidegger 1971b, 167). The thing, by contrast, is a 'going on', or better, a place where several goings on become entwined. To observe a thing is not to be locked out but to be invited in to the gathering.
>
> Ingold (2010, 4)

Ingold goes on to claim that things are in constant flow, constantly mutating and in contact with each other through their surfaces. Such a process of continuous mutation is intended to contrast with the notion of agency. According to Ingold, agency acts as a solution to resuscitate the otherwise 'dead' objects by giving them a sort of 'sprinkle' of life. Imagining the environment to be populated by objects suggests the image of an excavated world, similar to a piece of 'Swiss cheese' (Ingold 2011, 24). Ingold argues instead that things fill the environment and are entangled with one another, in 'a meshwork of interwoven lines of growth and movement' (Ingold 2010, 4).

The perspective offered by Ingold is more than an attempt to avoid a sort of *horror vacui* of an environment where objects are cut and surrounded by an empty space. There is still, for Ingold, the need to make sense of our own involvement, as things ourselves, participating in the world. For this reason, Ingold brings focus to the *life* of things. He writes: 'In effect, to render the life of things as the agency of objects is to effect a double reduction, of things to objects and of life to agency' (Ingold 2010, 7). Life is a crucial concept here for Ingold, and he explicitly mentions Bergson and his *Creative Evolution* as one of the major influences on his work (Ingold 2010, 13). From Bergson, Ingold develops the notion of life as movement and duration. To be alive, Ingold argues, means to participate in the generative fluxes and currents of a world of materials, and to join in their transformation. This participation is an act of retelling of the flows, mixtures and mutations of the materials that surround us.

Conclusion: Feeling Kinship with Video Games

How can my engagement with Nike+ FuelBand be retold, then? How could it possibly be transformed into something more *lively*? How can the idea of living with video games surpass the problems associated with the static understanding of engagement that gamification gurus propose? Ingold suggests that life is a process of involvement, of tying together the different elements and materials that surround us. It also requires that we acknowledge both intellectually and intuitively how different settings give rise to different relations and entities. If the world is made of connections, it matters which connections are made and unmade, as Donna Haraway puts it, and retelling my engagement with Nike's product will performatively reassemble the elements that make it relevant to me, at a given time (Haraway 1991). The connections I have been making (and unmaking) so far with Nike+ FuelBand give the impression that the engagement imagined in the development and marketing of gamification products is static and repetitive. The gadget itself is, after all, sold with the promise of providing a safe and certain knowledge about the quantification of movement, and not one that can ever be unsettled.

In the end, I have decided to break up with Nike+ FuelBand: our relationship, which was supposed to be, since its very beginning, focused around movement, was not really going anywhere. I do not know yet what our engagement will become, and I might as well continue having contradictory views on the role that should be played by Nike+ FuelBand in my life. (Should I use it occasionally? Should I resell it? Keep it in a drawer?). I do not yet know what to do with it. However, uncertainty could open the way for new possibilities: it is only through uncertainty and contradictions that an otherwise homogeneous engagement might become something other.

In conclusion, I propose that relationships with gamification, and more broadly with quantified selves, are thought of not in terms of engagement but in terms of *kinship*, as intended by Donna Haraway (2004, 2015). Following Haraway, kinship is open to uncertainty and to the possibility that relations might change, and possibly also end. Engagement, at least as it is understood by the gamification gurus, implies instead that time and space are homogeneous and predictable. Could there be a form of gamification that welcomes uncertain and catastrophic events which happen in time and cannot be undone? Could an experience be gamified in order to allow for the emergence of 'unstable and permanently partial identities and contradictory standpoints'? (Haraway 1991, 154). Gamification could also be interpreted to include interventions in the relationships between players and video games, which are personal, intuitive, timely and unique. At least, such an approach would contrast with the idea that gamification can improve users' lives by an absolute and transparent knowledge of their bodies and minds: knowledge itself would become unsettled, by introducing into engagement the possibility of its own mutation. Becoming kin with the games we play will introduce events into our gamified lives, producing a partial and strategic knowledge about ourselves and the games we play *with*.

Peter Krapp similarly argues that there is a difference between playing a game and playing *with* a game, as the latter means opening its commands and controls to critique and investigation (2011, 77). Playing with games, according to Krapp, is more than simply playing by the rules, and implies a less obedient approach to the ludic system. Krapp's notion echoes Alexander Galloway's 'countergaming' and his theory of creating 'gamic allegories', 'other-acts' or 'enacted metaphors' in the act of playing (2006, 104–6). However, I do not necessarily share their focus on action as the defining gesture of the player/critic. Both authors look at players' expected and possible actions as a key element in the understanding of how games work. Particularly in light of gamification, a trend which offers game environments that do not wait for the player's actions to keep functioning, I believe that these games are not necessarily systems to play against or 'counter', but rather ones that invite us to play in their company, as companions that are carried along (in pockets, on wrists, and so on). As perhaps a sign of a new stage of algorithmic culture, gamification does not produce allegories of life, but lively things. These games are not for playing with, but for living with.

Gamification could also be rethought as a different way of interpreting the title of Bogost's text *How to Do Things with Videogames*. 'With' could be rethought as 'in the company of', 'together with', rather than 'by using' video games: dwelling in video games, and living with them, rather than using them for a specific purpose. Gamified apps can remain static only so long as these are conceived of as tools, but they might also be interesting companions with which to do things together. Gamification, intended as the development of a relation of kinship with a video game, would force users to re-world and retell their own engagement and presence in the gamified environment, and to continuously redraw the boundaries, without knowing what could happen next.

Incidentally, this might also become a suggestion for those involved in the design and development of gamified apps and services. The expected engagement between users and games could be imagined as more similar to that of a romantic relationship, where both sides might change and influence each other radically, in ways that cannot be reversed. Can gamification also work while considering the mutations that happen in time, opening to movements of different kinds, and allowing uncertainty about what will happen in the future? That would be a different, more interesting, and surely far more pleasurable way of playing with one's (quantified) self. Gamification, seen by many commentators as the future of game design, could be interpreted as an anxious and ethical question about the relationships and negotiations between gamers and games, and their mutations in time. Gamification could also be seen less as a technique to frame user behaviour and more as a modality of creative invention and rewriting of alternative forms of cohabitation with digital games.

In the next chapter, I will look at how relations of kinship between humans and video games have been narrated by a certain number of actors who have recently been defined by specialists and gamers as independent game producers. In these contexts, being independent means being responsible for the conception, development and marketing of a video game. However, the definition of what independence really means, in video game culture, is disputed, and, as I will argue, the dispute is part and parcel of that destabilising uncertainty which makes these new forms of kinship significant. Independent video games have been featured at festivals, conferences and workshops, and have influenced new business models and modes of thinking about authorship in digital gaming for more than a decade. In the discourses surrounding this phenomenon, there seems to be a certain difficulty in explaining how the game developer should relate to his or her own work, and how making video games contributes to the identity of the developer. Independent developers are regularly invited to discuss what forms of relations take place when making, playing and thinking of a video game – and not just any video game, but one that is *their own*.

2

Independent Gaming: Take Care of Your Own Video Game

In the last decade, new discourses have been emerging that redefine the relationship between video games and their developers. In these discourses, replicated mostly by industry experts, journalists and gamers, and presented at conventions and conferences on gaming, the game designer has been re-evaluated as an *author*, that is, as someone who is solely responsible for the conception, development and release of a video game. The justification for the appraisal of this new figure has often been centred on technological change. Development tools such as Twine, Unity, Unreal Engine, RPG Maker and the now-dismissed Microsoft XNA have been seen as responsible for facilitating the production of games. Thanks to these freely available tools, an individual could supposedly decide to give up a job in the industry and become a video game author, or learn from scratch how to make a game. In 2015 the companies behind the most commonly used development tools in the industry, Unity and the Unreal Engine, decided to follow the trend and release their software for free, asking to be paid only when the user reaches a certain amount of earnings. At least in theory, anyone can now download the same tools used by the largest video game companies and use them to make and release a digital game. Although discourses around authorship in game development are not entirely new, they have re-emerged in recent years, applying a deterministic view of software, which is now seen as being capable of redefining the present and future of the video game industry.

Indeed, the appearance of new forms of video game production and new modes of organisation of the development cycle are not due only to the release of free software packages. Discourses from the creative industries, where the individual is now seen as an entrepreneur in the fashion, cinema or music industries, have provided a framework for the idea of the game author. Since its early years, the video game industry has generally conformed to patterns of production and publishing established in other cultural and creative industries (Kerr 2006, 43–74; Hesmondhalgh 2013, 358–62). Likewise, the emergence of individual developers and small companies appears to replicate what has already happened in other sectors.

This change in the understanding of the relation between a video game producer and his or her video game product is often narrated in terms of *independence*. Many creative industries (film, music, fashion, and so on), where the previous conditions of work allowed only large companies to participate, are now welcoming independent individuals or groups who work in the field part or full time. Video game culture has seen a similar acceptance of the alleged benefits of becoming an independent producer. In the context of video game culture, independence generally refers to the possibility of financing, developing and releasing a video game independently of a mainstream publisher, that is, by marking the difference between oneself, or a relatively close group to which one belongs, and the broader digital entertainment industry. Such a new form of self-organisation is expected to bring benefits to whoever decides to work outside the mainstream industry. The developer can in fact work at his or her own pace while experimenting with new forms of design, controlling the production process from beginning to end and potentially receiving, on top of personal satisfaction, all revenues from sales or in-game advertising. In this view, independence is the result not just of a changing technological paradigm but also of personal research into self-expression or a more remunerative business model.

However, the liberating effects of independence are often disputed. Mainstream publishers have quickly appropriated some of the channels of digital distribution, offering game producers visibility within these spaces and, consequently, higher revenues. This has reintroduced, for many independents, relations of power and control that were already in place in the previous, non-independent condition of work. Valve's Steam online network is, for many, the only place where it is possible to reach a significant audience. However, this is a controlled space, owned by one of the largest video game publishers, which takes around 30 percent of the total revenues for offering visibility to independent game makers.[1]

Nowadays, independence appears to mean very different things to those who profess to be part of it. For many game developers aiming to receive attention and visibility on distribution channels controlled by new or pre-existing publishers, independence appears as a different way of organising work, taking sole responsibility for a larger and more diverse number of issues (game concepts, programming, storyline, budgets, and so on) that would ordinarily be assigned to specialised personnel within non-independent forms of production. In this understanding, independence appears as a new mode of work management (Martin and Deuze 2009). For others, independence mostly constitutes the opportunity to express themselves outside the logic of the market, releasing games for free and claiming a larger degree of freedom in the choice of a game's content and style.

The interpretations that game developers give of their relationships with their own games are rich with contradictions and complexities (Guevara-Villalobos 2015). Reports by the industry expert Brendan Sinclair on GameIndustry.biz (a website for news and trends on the business side of gaming) have highlighted the disappointments and frustrations of those who decided to become independents. On 31 March 2016, an exhaustive interview with indie designer Joshua Boggs shows how the search for independence can sometimes be driven by an unhealthy and self-destructive vanity. Boggs recalls how the myth of the author led him to conflicts with his own team, and how the fear of disappointing himself and those who supported his work led him to suffer from periods of severe anxiety. As he argues in the interview, the constant attention he received was for him like a drug, and he always needed more to keep going. The spiral was fuelled by being at the front of the project, connected to his own game both intimately and publicly: 'the independent scene, it's always names and faces. The success of your game is often tied to you as a person, so what we end up doing is putting all our self-worth in it' (Sinclair 2016a). In

---

[1] Alternative models such as Itch.io, where games can be exchanged without paying shares to the owners of the online platform, can be seen as a direct response to the dominance of Steam in the distribution of independent games.

another interview with Tim Dawson, developer for the indie game *Assault Android Cactus*, Sinclair highlights the developer's feelings of inadequacy and the fear of not being good enough to accomplish what he promised to those who backed the project on Kickstarter. The relationship with the game is presented as one of paranoia and conflict, fuelled by fear of not receiving the necessary attention to make his work successful, or simply not delivering what he promised to himself and to the players (Sinclair 2016b).

Feelings of inadequacy and anxiety, along with accomplishment and self-fulfilment, all seem to appear around a mesh of diverse and contradictory discourses where the relationship with one's own video game is placed at the centre. While critics of this concept claim that being independent might not mean anything in particular in the video game industry today, precisely because of the large variety of inconsistent practices and games labelled as such, I will argue that the notion could still be of use to video game culture. As an academic and gamer, I believe the novelty of the concept is not to be hastily dismissed, for it might yet generate valuable creative interventions. As I will argue, independence might be interesting less as a model for the future of game development, than as a key concept for understanding the fluctuating and contradictory relationships that developers have with their own work in the present. Independent developers intervene in game culture by writing and talking about video games, and in so doing they write and talk about themselves and their own relationship with the product of their work.

While many have tried to define what independence actually means or whether independent games have a defining style that makes them unique, in this chapter I would like to offer a slightly different perspective by looking at the difficulty per se of such a definition (Lipkin 2013; Juul 2014). I argue that independence can be seen as a simultaneously repressive and productive concept, which forces game developers to confront their own definitions and positions in relation to their own game and to other forms of independence and non-independence. As I will show below, the need to answer the question of what is meant by independence performs a double function. On the one hand, it reduces the possibilities of what should count as independent, establishing boundaries around this notion so as to include and exclude specific practices. On the other, it produces the notion of independence and the idea of the independent game developer, giving it a clearer set of characteristic duties and responsibilities.

However, the irremediable impossibility of defining what independence truly means, for anyone and at any single point in time, means that the concept provides interesting grounds for the introduction of a novel question on the *ethics* of gaming. Indeed, at stake in these issues is much more than the understanding of a phenomenon of video game culture: the ways in which independence is currently being discussed in this field could offer insights into how independence is more broadly interpreted as a political concept. Independence is often discussed by those involved as a self-imposed imperative to do *well*: to take care of one's own game and its players. Anxieties and uncertainties are often approached in the name of an ethics of independence, and the emergence of statements and events that explicitly refer to this new ethos of game development constitutes an original aspect of contemporary game culture. Moreover, the use of independence to define the relations between different actors and the outcome of their work can shed light on how the relation with media and technologies is also interpreted by the actors involved. I will address these points by looking at the conflicts between the independents and the so-called professional industry, where those who are not independent work and fulfil their lives.

Trying Not to Be Professional

Apart from a few accounts that look at those who are discontented with the emergence of independent forms of game production, the phenomenon is most often narrated in a celebratory tone. In most cases the perspective is on the relation between the new independent scene and the world of professional, institutionalised game production. For example, this is how independent gaming is described in the documentary *Indie Game: The Movie* (2012) by James Swirsky and Lisanne Pajot. In this documentary, well received by critics and awarded the prize for best World Cinema Documentary Editing at the 2012 Sundance Film Festival, the directors interview four of the most celebrated independent developers: Jonathan Blow, author of the game *Braid* (2008); Edmund McMillen and Tommy

Refenes, authors of *Super Meat Boy* (2010); and Phil Fish, author of *Fez* (2012). The directors celebrate, through their interviews, the changes wrought by independent gaming and, in particular, the emotional attachment that independents have to their games. This attachment, according to the documentary, has begun to diminish in recent major productions, where much larger budgets and numbers of developers are now required. In mainstream productions, according to this narrative, it is necessary to cover the initial input by trying to appeal to an overly broad audience. Meanwhile, the production process is broken down into undistinguished, mechanical tasks. In the same documentary, mainstream productions are presented as being too polished and lacking in personality. Independent games represent, in the narrative replicated by those interviewed by Swirsky and Pajot, a sort of new opportunity where game designers are now finally free to express themselves as authors of their own work. In the words of independent designer Jonathan Blow:

> Part of it is trying not to be professional. A lot of people come into indie games trying to be like a big company. What those game companies do is create highly polished things that serve as large as an audience as possible. The way that you do that is by filing off all the bumps on something. If there is a sharp corner you make sure it is not going to hurt anybody if they bump into it or whatever. That creation of this highly glossy commercial product is the opposite of making something personal.
>
> *Indie Game: The Movie* (2012)

However, there are also different and co-existing interpretations of how independence relates to the mainstream game industry. Some game designers define themselves as radical independents functioning in an antagonistic relationship not only with the video game industry but also with the more famous indies popularised by game conventions, magazines and documentaries, such as Swirsky and Pajot's. According to these other independents, designers such as those interviewed in *Indie Game: The Movie* represent a sort of polished version of independence as they tend to replicate the same system of production and publishing as that embraced by mainstream productions, only on a smaller scale.

An example of this understanding of independence can be seen in the collective Molleindustria, who define their works on their website as 'radical games against the tyranny of entertainment' (Molleindustria 2016). Molleindustria view game design as a political practice for activism and social critique (Ruffino 2015). Their games are not commercially released and are available for free on their website. Molleindustria's games usually articulate a political standpoint. Examples of this are *McDonald's Videogame* (2006), a game about the unsustainable business of food corporations, *Oiligarchy* (2008), a critique of the exploitation of natural resources, *Operation: Pedopriest* (2007), about the Vatican sex scandal, and *Unmanned* (2012), a game about the life of a drone pilot in the US Air Force.

Moreover, the founder and main spokesperson of the group, Paolo Pedercini, has publicly expressed his view on independent gaming on many occasions. In a talk at the game conference IndieCade, Pedercini argued that independent designers cannot consider themselves properly autonomous. According to Pedercini, the reappropriation of independent productions operated by some of the major video game publishers undermines the freedom of the developers. Pedercini further suggests that we need to rethink how best to pursue independence, while recognising the impossibility of attaining it in its purest form, as well as how different forms of independence could (and in fact do) co-exist and should be supported. As he put it himself at the 2012 IndieCade conference:

There are a lot of people these days trying to come up with new definitions of independent development that take into account the various degrees of autonomy from platform owners and hardware manufacturers; the co-optation of styles, keywords and modes that used to be part of the 'indie' identity; and the mainstream acceptance and structural expansion of the most successful independent developers.

Pedercini (2012, online)

He suggests in the same speech that independence is considered a spectrum whose extremes are, at one end, a sort of unreachable utopian autarchy and, at its opposite, a completely dehumanised activity where the worker does what he or she is told, with no emotional involvement in the final outcome. Pedercini argues that the utopian idea of complete independence can never be fully achieved but can nonetheless frame the practice of those game designers who aim to reach it.

In fact, major publishers have attempted to appropriate independent productions in recent years, further complicating the debate on what should count as independence. The games presented in *Indie Game: The Movie*, as well as many of the most popular independent games and the movie itself, are on sale on the online markets of game publishers Valve and Microsoft, which are hardly grassroots companies or at the margins of the game industry. Recently, these two game publishers have promoted the indie channels of their online platforms for digital distribution (respectively, Steam and Xbox Live). The presence of these distributors has shaped a sort of alternative video game industry, running parallel to the mainstream one. Individual or small groups of game developers design and promote video games in the hope of being offered the possibility of featuring on the indie channels of Valve or Microsoft, where they are sold next to the major productions of the game industry. Conceding part of the revenue is deemed acceptable by these developers, who are often confronted with an increasing number of small-scale competitors and with the associated difficulties of competing against them in an open online market. Pedercini's argument appears to be a reasonable description of some of the current developments within the independent sector: the emerging practice of substituting the previous employers with new gatekeepers such as Valve and Microsoft can be seen to undermine some of the claims of independence. Furthermore, the new gatekeepers have a determining power with regard to which games will reach a sufficient audience and therefore be able to cover the initial investment and hence finance future projects.

However, the new conditions of precariousness do not seem to adversely affect the enthusiastic claims in favour of independent gaming. The documentary *Indie Game: The Movie* begins by showing the developer Tommy Refenes looking desperate in front of the homepage of Microsoft XBox Live because it is not displaying his most recent game, as had been agreed with the publisher. Despite the designer describing this mistake by Microsoft as a matter of life and death for his independent career, it does not hinder, throughout the rest of the documentary, the celebration of independent gaming as a form of liberation for video game developers.

More recent debates within gamer communities have suggested that perhaps the label independent should be replaced by a more specific denomination. *Gamespot* contributor Tom McShea has argued in a popular article that 'indie has become a term as nebulous as it is ubiquitous . . . It's time we put these categorisations to rest' (McShea 2014). Several days later on the same website, Alex Newhouse replied with an article claiming instead that we should not 'throw "indie" away just yet', as it is the only word to designate games in which the personalities of the authors 'shine through' (Newhouse 2014). In fact, the debate on the real meaning of independence in the context of video game culture has run parallel to the emergence of autonomous forms of video game development. In 2002, game designer and researcher Eric Zimmerman was already questioning whether truly independent games really exist (Zimmerman 2002). In any case, the lack of an agreed definition has done little to slow down the practitioners of independent gaming and the emergence of festivals, incubators for new companies, articles and awards centred round this phenomenon. Quite the contrary. The phenomenon is increasing in size and new institutions continue to be formed.

I believe that it is precisely this undefined condition that stimulates the need to produce definitions of the concept of independence. These are often self-definitions, produced by game developers as they try to position themselves in relation to the existent independent scene. Furthermore, the reappropriation of the indie label by the mainstream industry highlights the difficulty of understanding what a radical outside to the discourses of independence could be: to what extent is it possible to talk about such acts as forms of appropriation or reappropriation rather than seeing them as forms of the actual production of independence?

Independent game production appears to be stuck in this moment of negotiation where, by trying 'not to be professional', as Blow put it, the main actors are constantly pushed to define what it means to be professional and what might be a *good* way of *not* being professional. Indeed, many of these modalities of not being professional might now be the standard, or the new professional, as crowdfunding, micropayments and online distribution are common practice for productions of any magnitude. However, precisely because the practices that once belonged to independent game production might have become the new normal, it is vitally important to question where they might take us.

Too Short a Blanket: The Productive Potential of Independence

Independence may appear in video game culture as a blanket that is too short: pulling it in one direction may reveal a gap in the other, leaving some self-professed independents out in the cold. However, it is also as scarce as it is necessary. Independence is not just a label that one may choose to adopt for oneself; it is also productive of that very same notion of the self.

Through the work of Michel Foucault, I intend to consider independence as a productive force, precisely because of its floating condition (Foucault 1977, 1978, 1980, 78–108).[2] Foucault theorised that language is not just descriptive of reality but constitutive of it, and also of the very subjects of discourse. To summarise a large theoretical work, it could be said that, according to Foucault, when the world is described through language, it is not only given a structure; at the same time, our position and the position of others is also framed within that structure. From his perspective, talking about independence in video game culture – more specifically, by saying things that are considered 'true' – brings about the very concept of independence. Consequently, the position of the independent developer is also framed within those discourses as an imagined subject who embodies the values of independence. For the game developer who has decided to make and release his or her own game, the notion becomes a driving force to differentiate him- or herself and to understand what it is that makes that product personal and unique in contrast to the undifferentiated outside of independence.

From this perspective, independence becomes an enticement to a discourse of self-definition, a regulatory frame that produces the need to define and locate oneself in relation to this continuum. In Foucauldian terms, independence could be seen as a concept around which one organises a practice of care of the self. As Foucault argues: 'the care of oneself is a sort of thorn which must be stuck in men's flesh, driven into their existence, and which is a principle of restlessness and movement, of continuous

---

[2] The relation between power and knowledge is indeed central to the work of Michel Foucault, and will be addressed in the rest of this chapter through a variety of sources. In particular, the notion is well explained and summarised in the lecture he gave on 14 January 1976 at the College de France, collected in the text *Power/Knowledge: Selected Interviews and Other Writings 1972–1977*, edited by Gordon Colin (1980, New York: Pantheon).

concern throughout life' (2005, 8). The techniques of knowledge of the self, analysed by Foucault with respect to Greek and Roman times, and later with respect to Christian and contemporary culture, construct the possibility of arriving at and articulating the truth about oneself. The power of these discourses consists in their production of the individual, by fixating and naming the things that the individual has or has not done, and should or should not do. On this account, the discursive articulation of independence and non-independence can be seen as immediately productive of discourses and performances, and the productivity of such a binary lies in the latter's unresolvable condition. As there is no solution to the problem of defining what it means to become independent, there is no end to the potential productivity of this concept and no final resolution to the quest for independence (just as in the Foucauldian understanding of the care of the self, the *epimeleia heautou*, there is no method to test when complete self-sufficiency has been reached, or when sanctity has been achieved).

The indie channels on Steam and Xbox Live, or the sponsoring of independent festivals by mainstream companies, can be seen as producing, in their own turn, further definitions of independence, rather than being just belated attempts to exploit a pre-existing phenomenon. This process of moving and contesting the boundaries of independence is, I suggest, what constitutes independent gaming: it produces and incites verbal performances; it facilitates the production of games, events, articles and festivals, as well as forms of hospitality (such as inviting gamers to play for free or inviting designers to distribute their games through dedicated online channels), all of which contribute to defining who and what is included in the independent territory. In the next section, I will examine the discursive performances through which the definition of independence emerges, and when its boundary is drawn to separate it from the alleged other side of the non-independent territory.

The Outside of Independence

Independent game developers often discuss what it is that makes them different from the mainstream industry. This mostly happens in interviews, public speeches and personal statements. Finding this element of difference is one of the discursive strategies used in order to construct their own individualisation. For example, independent developer Jonatan Söderström, also known as Cactus, became particularly well known in the independent games community for his ability to design and release a video game in no more than a couple of days. He is celebrated by the likes of the Independent Games Festival, where he was nominated in 2008 (Excellence in Visual Arts and Excellence in Audio with the game *Clean Asia!*) and won in 2010 (Nuovo Award with the game *Tuning*). When he received the Nuovo Award, given in the category of original visual design, he remained silent on the stage for some time, sipped some water, and finally thanked 'Jesus [and God] for the inspiration to make this game.'[3] With this intentionally irreverent presentation, Cactus provided an anti-climactic moment of bathos that clashed with the declamatory style of the award ceremony as a whole. Cactus marks his distance not only from the so-called mainstream but also from other independent designers such as Jonathan Blow, who instead appear as much more conformist in their attitudes to the established industry. Cactus marks his own difference through a variety of actions. His refusal to work for a stable company or to publish his games anywhere other than on his own website has led to him being viewed as a representative of the advocates of pure indie gaming. Not coincidentally, when Cactus worked on his first commercially released game, *Hotline Miami* (2012), developed in collaboration with Dennis Wedin, he was asked to explain the decision. In an interview published a few weeks before the release of the game, he claims that someone suggested he contact publisher Digital Devolver after seeing the demo, and that working for a commercially released game pushed him to 'try to be a bit more *polished*' (Procter 2012) – the same word used by Jonathan Blow to define professionally produced video games.

Claiming an irreducible difference from other developers places Cactus in an individualistic territory, where conventional rules do not apply. However, the risk of claiming an absolute particularism is to relegate oneself to the periphery – a sort of self-ghettoisation. This way of presenting oneself is also representative of an ethos, a way of working and

---

[3] The award ceremony and Cactus's speech can be seen on YouTube, 'IGF Awards 2010 Part 2/2', min. 4'00"–5'58". www.youtube.com/watch?v=EDVZg9kZXEY (last accessed 29 January 2017).

living, in which every action (including the games produced) must some-how communicate a divergence from the standards of the industry and from what is expected from a video game. Through the creation of his own particularism, Cactus also claims a radical separation, presenting himself and his video games as incompatible with the outside of his own limited territory.

The production of the independent territory happens as much through the production of video games as it does through the use of language, and it involves statements that situate the independent developer within the world. Thus, these acts of self-definition can also be evaluated from the standpoint of political theory, as they too seek to interpret the surrounding world and provide justifications for emancipating oneself from it. Ernesto Laclau looks at how emancipation is typically defined through a binary opposition between universalism and particularism (Laclau 1996). I turn to the work of Laclau because of his attention to language and discourse in framing social and cultural phenomena. Laclau is interested in the con-flicts and processes of antagonism that are undertaken through discourse, and how identities are created in the process of relating to 'floating' or 'empty' signifiers: ideas such as 'the West', 'democracy', or, we could say, 'independence', which are never fully defined (Laclau 1990, 28; 1993, 287). In his work, contextualising one's position in relation to a floating signifier is a linguistic performance that implies a political negotiation, as it defines one's position in relation to others. Claims of belonging to a particular and emancipated group, for instance, often deny the presence of connections and relations between external groups.

Distancing oneself from concepts, practices and other human beings necessarily creates connections with those same signifiers that are other-wise repudiated. While analysing the concept of apartheid, Laclau argues that 'if the oppressed is defined by its difference from the oppressor, such a difference is an essential component of the identity of the oppressed' (1996, 29). Each particular group necessarily belongs, at the same time, to the universal sphere that they might otherwise neglect. The problem with radical separation is not really the act of separation per se, but how such an act effectively creates the other, the opposite side from which one is to be separated. I propose that the key issue here is: what sort of outside is formulated in shaping these radically independent identities? Laclau continues: '[the oppressed] cannot assert its identity without assert-ing that of the oppressor as well' (1996, 29). Oppression need not entail physical coercion; it can be a limiting power and, in Foucauldian terms, is always already productive. What comes to be produced is not only the independent territory but also its outside, which often appears as a uni-form, coercive force (i.e. an undifferentiated side, where the economic, social, cultural and political aspects involved in the production of a video game are predictable and imposed on the workers).

A further development of this approach, I argue, would be to consider the production of video games as involving a multiplicity of particular approaches, none of them single-handedly constituting the independent and non-independent realm. Rather, each delineates, in its own way, an element of difference. This approach, however, comes at the cost of reanalysing not only independence as a plurality of forms but also non-independence in its multiple variations. In other words, it would entail a redefinition of the very distinction between the two sides as a multi-plicity of different practices of production, not completely consistent or equal to each other but mutually defining one another through a process of self-differentiation. Thus, the particularism and uniqueness evoked by many independent developers with regard to their own practice should be looked at closely, as much as the universalism that is assumed to belong to the *others* of these discourses of self-definition. Both particularisms and universalisms need to be unpacked in their apparent unity.

As Laura Zerilli points out, reflecting on Laclau's political theory: 'uni-versalism is not One: it is not a pre-existing something (essence or form) to which individuals accede but, rather, the fragile, shifting, and always incomplete achievement of political action; it is not the container of a presence but the placeholder of an absence, not a substantive content but an empty place' (2006, 102). For instance, in Molleindustria's talk at IndieCade, independence is imagined as a spectrum that ranges from the least to the most independent forms of game production (Pedercini 2012). However, Pedercini's view does not suggest the presence of a further out-side in the continuum between independence and non-independence. In his view, each game developer is potentially involved in this continuum, which means that anyone who is involved in the production of a video game could be assessed according to his or her degree of independence (and non-independence). Thus, the definition of where one is on the continuum precedes the understanding of how the subject is situated in relation to the 'fragile', universal other. I believe that the order should be reversed: the relation with the absent-other is at the foundation of the very possibility of defining oneself as (more or less) independent, and such a relation precedes the possibility of a self-definition. I argue that independence should be understood as implying its own opposite, its own outside: a shifting and incomplete form of *otherness* to take into account, and which pre-exists the claim of independence.

It has often been argued that independent gaming recalls previous forms of video game production, such as the phenomenon of the bedroom coders, who were programming video games in the 1980s and 1990s individually or in small teams, and reselling their work to major publishers when completed (Foddy 2014). However, it can be seen here that a difference is starting to emerge, one that makes the contemporary trend of independent production rather different from other forms of game development. The difference consists in how the independent developer is brought to explain, define and justify his or her independence, and how, while doing so, they are also shaping the image of a universal other. But that universal is not singular: it is composed of people, games and practices of production that can sometimes be thought of as too professional and polished to be indie, and sometimes, in other circumstances, instead be re-evaluated and included in a broader definition of independence.

The drawing of these shifting boundaries between the individual singular and the universal other appears often as a regulated practice, made of workshops and incubators where game developers are trained to think of themselves as independents and to be able to draw the boundary. The abundance of these almost educational contexts offers occasions to look at how precisely the constitution of a boundary between the first person and the others is solicited, curated and evaluated, and with what consequences.

Independence as Regulated Practice

Recent years have seen the rise of several contexts where presentations, workshops and meetings are organised to provide guidelines and suggestions to video game developers who want to be independent. On these occasions an expert or consultant usually provides instructional material on how to express oneself in a personal and unique form through a video game. This process involves advertising, communication with the press, direct contact with the audience through social networks, management of intellectual properties, relations with online distributors, and more issues focused on the economic sustainability of independent companies. These services satisfy the demand to overcome the increasing competition among developers in the independent sector, where introducing a new product is relatively easy in economic terms. However, I believe there is a more pressing issue at stake here for the developers, apart from gaining the necessary visibility to sell a video game product. This sort of training focuses not only on how to market an independent video game but also on how to ensure it can be classed as independent.

What comes to be associated with independence is often a series of provisions and limitations on which actions are to be performed in order for a game designer to become independent. These often take the form of operational procedures, a series of dos and don'ts, lists and instructions. This process of becoming independent therefore appears to include not only verbal performances but also certain practical and operational behaviours. Independence comes to stimulate a need or desire (or probably a need to desire – the necessity of feeling attracted) to be in control of one's own production. This solicitation also produces specific contexts where the drive to become independent is seen as an operation that can be taught.

As I will discuss shortly in relation to Execution Labs and the Indie Dev Day at the Develop convention, this and other similar institutions provide a 'technology of the self' that is grounded in the idea that game designers have an identity to express in their video games (Foucault 1998). In this narrative, expressing one's own self is what a designer should desire. However, in order to be successful the desire might need to be instructed through specific techniques. The individual plays a significant role in these narratives of independent gaming, as an actor who brings an element of their own personality to the final product. More importantly, in these examples the relation between producer and product comes to constitute the object of a form of knowledge. Some of the institutionalised practices that are now emerging in independent gaming are operating at both a conceptual and a practical level to create an institutionalised path to becoming independent. Such practices therefore come to constitute a further articulation of a more general self-regulatory practice, where the emergence of a different market and production process of video games materialises and is grounded in the constitution of individual identities, and of institutions where one can learn how to become this kind of independent individual.

The Execution Labs project, founded in Montreal, Canada, in 2012 and begun in January 2013, is one of the latest and major examples. Execution Labs presents itself as an institution that knows how to channel ambition and personal motivation in the right direction and towards independence. In this narrative, creativity has to be regulated in order to become productive and marketable. Once this process is completed, independence is supposedly achieved. The forms of mentoring and consultancy that Execution Labs offers are therefore oriented towards the regulation of the self, making a business out of the capacity to communicate personal creativity through a video game. The main service offered by Execution Labs is assistance in regulating the constitution of a particularism, a difference from the universal context, which the independent subject then has to market to the community of video game players.

The production of the independent subject appears quite explicitly in some of the keynotes and presentations for aspiring independent developers. Eric Zimmerman has offered his own method to become a *good* independent developer when presenting at several institutions (including the aforementioned Execution Labs) for game designers and industry practitioners. At IndieCade 2012 he gave a presentation on 'being a game designer: principles for a thoughtful practice' (IndieCade 2012). Zimmerman introduces his lecture thus:

Most talks on games focus on how to make a better product – a more successful game. This session frames what game designers do in a different way. I want to ask the question: What does it mean to be a good game designer? . . . Is it possible to think about game design as a way or mode of being? . . . This is not meant as a 'theoretical' talk that focuses on abstract design concepts, but is intended as more of a personal meditation. Rather than thinking about how to make great games, and how those games can transform our players' lives, I'd like to ask how it is that making games can transform their designers.

IndieCade (2012)

Such practice of self-transformation is regulated through a process of knowledge, where the developer must learn to be honest about what the game truly is, and to understand what he or she truly wants.

Similar events also take place in Europe and the United Kingdom. One of the most prominent events for independent game designers is the Indie Dev Day, which takes place in Brighton, UK, during the Develop conference, addressed to the mainstream industry. On 11 July 2012, independent designer Michael Movel from game company Fat Pebble delivered a presentation addressed to independent developers. Interestingly, his case is particularly complicated because of a commercial agreement he made with Zynga, one of the biggest publishers of online video games aimed at a casual audience, which offered to curate the marketing of Movel's games. Despite this agreement, Movel explains how and why his work should be considered independent. According to Movel, an indie developer is someone who creates his or her own game, has creative control and cares about the quality of the final product. Movel argues that the absence of a marketing department is one of the three most important 'indie power-ups', the other two being the absence of any restraint ('you are free to push the boundaries, you don't have to make another First-Person Shooter or strategy game'), and individual passion, which contributes to the differentiation of each product (Movel 2012). The absence of a marketing department is also one of the greatest challenges, according to Movel. However, in his specific case, Zynga had stepped in during the production process to curate the marketing of the game. Movel points out that, despite the intervention of a publisher, he has full creative control and should therefore be considered independent.

Movel then explains how, precisely, a video game should be marketed, presenting it as the result of a personal, almost intimate process. Part of the marketing takes place on social networks such as Twitter, where the independent designer is expected to present the game and narrate the production process itself, engaging in discussions with the potential players (and buyers) of the game. These comments are supposed to show the developer at work, while struggling to reach the final stages of the production process and communicating the personal fatigue of taking care of the whole process on one's own.

This process is regulated through a precise technique, where the number of tweets to deliver each day, the press releases and the preview videos are predetermined. They have to be consistent and engage the audience. The process is so precise that it can be handed over to a professional company, as happened to Movel with Zynga. Such a precise communication, and the option of outsourcing it to a separate company, does not undermine, according to Movel, the claims of freedom and self-expression often associated with independence. What is communicated is still a very personal and individual perspective, a passionate understanding of game design, despite this communication being strongly calculated, almost numbered.

Independent gaming, in this more recent development, involves the emergence of practical organisational techniques, such as application forms, workshops and incubators. While this way of approaching the notion of independence does not bring us to an explicit understanding of what independence is, it does provide explanations as to how one can be independent, and where independence should be negotiated. On these occasions the process of becoming independent is transformed into the object of knowledge. Independence here becomes a *methodology* for the creation of difference and particularity.

The question I would like to pose, in the conclusion, relates to how such a methodology could be evaluated beyond its effectiveness in guaranteeing autonomy to a game developer. I would like to question the possibility of introducing different criteria for deciding when independence is also what might be called a *good* independence (as Zimmerman similarly suggests in his talk at IndieCade 2012). Incubators and workshops teach game developers how to do well in terms of the economic feasibility of their projects, the content and marketing of their work as independent. But how else can the practice of taking care of one's own video game become, in the context of video game culture, a *good methodology*? What other standards could be introduced in deciding how to be a good independent? The question shares some features with those questions posed at numerous festivals, incubators and workshops: these events analyse the quality of a video game and ask whether the developer can truly be considered independent. However, if one has to take *ethically* the question of what constitutes good independence, then other criteria for its evaluation will have to be introduced, aside from the economic and artistic ones.

This ethical question is precisely what makes independent gaming important at present. By introducing the problem of evaluating one's relation with the others and with one's own work, it demonstrates that it is not just a model for the future of game development but is a challenge to the contemporary categories of the game industry. In the final part of this chapter, I will argue that independence might also become an ethical practice, precisely because of its undetermined condition and necessity to include a confrontation with an otherness in the form of the rest of the video game industry or other independent developers.

Conclusion: Independence as Ethics

In this chapter I have tried to read and intervene *creatively* within the study of independent forms of game development by looking at the authorities that define the notion of independence, the performative function of statements produced by independent developers, and their own anxious involvement in a field that mutates in time as they talk about it. In the final part I want to focus on the notion of ethics. If independence implies the drawing of boundaries and differences, then the sources of authority and legitimation and the criteria that make certain boundaries thicker than others could be critiqued. The linguistic performances that negotiate boundaries between oneself and the outside, the independent territory and the non-independent other, frame and bring both sides into being. The statements produced by independent developers have the effect of opening and constraining the possibilities of independence: these statements are enunciated in and define the present, but they also argue about what the present might become, and what one could do as an independent. The process of defining oneself in relation to others is immediately operational, as it produces video games, festivals, incubators, articles and interviews. The issue I want to investigate in the conclusion to this chapter is how to evaluate this incessant production of independent territories. The notion of independence is often discussed by those involved as personal choice and a method for taking care of games and gamers, a way of working and living that is *better* than that of the non-independents.

Independent game design introduces novel questions in relation to the production of video games. Developers do not just produce a video game; they also produce themselves: their own definition and difference from the others. This practice represents a re-evaluation of the practice of game development seen as necessarily entwined with a reflection on one's own presence in the world. What is involved in this modus operandi as it becomes a general modus vivendi? As proposed by Richard Sennett in *The Craftsman*, in relation to Hannah Arendt, the practice of knowing oneself through a working practice can also become a form of politics, a means to know what you are doing (Sennett 2008; Arendt 1958).

Joanna Zylinska, in *Bioethics in the Age of New Media*, discusses similar forms of self-management with regard to the phenomenon of blogging. Bloggers can be seen as being part of a larger 'neo/liberal imperative for individualized productivity', but they can also be questioned with regard to the forms of hospitality that this individualisation entails (Zylinska 2009, 96). Individualisation 'necessarily' becomes a form of narcissism but, as Zylinska asks, to what extent could it be re-evaluated as an ethical narcissism, 'one which is more open to the experience of the other as other' (2009, 88)?

Being an independent game designer could become a way of doing games through the ethical question of taking care of the other, of the non-independent or the diversely independent, the other forms of independence which-are-not-mine. This other, as I have argued, is always and necessarily there; he, she or it is intrinsic to the notion of independence. It can be the other to be separated from (the mainstream industry, for instance) or the other who has alternative and incompatible definitions of independence (the small company that makes clones of mobile games and the solo artist can both call themselves independent, while disagreeing with each other's definition of independence). What independent gaming is introducing into video game culture is more than an alleged revolution in the management of game production, or in the broadening of the availability of the means to make and publish a game. Its most original aspect rather lies in the need for game designers to relate themselves to a form of otherness, to make this relation explicit and give it a certain value.

As Zylinska argues, through Emmanuel Levinas, the infinite 'alterity' of the other and its undecidability are at the foundation of discourse (Zylinska 2005, 14). Discourse needs confirmation by way of an interlocutor, or in a form of otherness that confronts, evaluates and judges it.

Independent gaming shows us that even the highest level of narcissism and separation from a more or less imaginary mainstream context, precisely because of this act of separation, needs to confront a form of otherness. The difficulty that independence poses, therefore, is in how this otherness is accounted for, taken care of and hosted. How, to what extent and with what consequences can the narcissism of certain kinds of independent video game design remain open to such otherness and also become an ethical game design?

The most pressing question I have tried to approach is how diverse claims of independence come to constitute a practice for the definition of the identity of video game producers. From this perspective, it seems to me that independent gaming is a name given to a set of discursive practices related to the production of a video game through which the game developer seeks to answer the question, 'Who am I?'. I am generalising here about a phenomenon that I have tried, so far, to keep united in its multiple forms. But if a unifying proposition had to be found, for the sake of a summarising and conclusive note, then I believe that this quest to define oneself is what characterises independent gaming. More than a practice of production of video games, it appears to be mostly a practice of production of the self.

Moreover, the incessant emergence of discourses that attempt to describe what independent gaming is, how to be part of it and also how to succeed and make a living out of it, could also be reinterpreted as not only a practice of self-production on the part of the game developers but as a way to avoid, so to speak, self-consumption, or self-destruction. The risk of not regulating the self, not emerging as a defined first-person singular, could come at the cost of disappearing in an undefined universalism 'which is not one' (Zerilli 2006).

Indeed, this also seems to be part of the anxiety inherent in the self-exploitative regimes that some independent developers fall into. In the documentary *Indie Game: The Movie* there is a moment when this appears, I believe, quite clearly. It is when designer Phil Fish, developer of the game *Fez*, narrates his own personal story. The difficulties he is facing in concluding the video game are not only economic but existential:

The game has become a bit of a reflection of me over time. It certainly wasn't the intention at first . . . and now we're here. We don't have any money. I'm overworked and over-stressed. I'm on the line. Me. My name . . . my career. If this fails,

I'm done. I don't think I'll work in games again. And it's not just a game, I'm so closely attached to it. It's me. It's my ego, my perception of myself is at risk. This is my identity: Fez. I'm guy [sic] making Fez. That's about it. If that doesn't work out then . . . I would kill myself. I would kill myself. That's my incentive to finish it. Because then I get to not kill myself.

Indie Game: The Movie (2012)

Narcissism can turn into solipsism, and when the only thing that matters for the independent developer is the game he or she is making, then, at the risk of making too big a statement, life itself can be under threat, as there is no form of otherness to account for or through which to seek confirmation. Independence forces one to look for different others. It appears as a need to trace the boundary of one's own independence, as well as to look for contamination and similarity, to find other independents that can attribute value to an otherwise isolated work. Independence can be a repressive power that forces one to say what one *is not*, but it is also productive. It produces alterity in the first place, and movement towards the other.

I have looked at authoritarian speech acts that define and perform the notion of independence. However, I have also argued that the concept is always undoing itself, as it requires the existence of an absent-other that is invented through the same act of defining one's own independence. Many commentators discuss the future of independence, asking if it still has value today, and if it will ever guarantee to its participants a satisfactory form of emancipation. I argue that these visions of the possibilities of independent gaming are constructed in the present: the undecidability of the concept puts the speaker in an anxious state where he or she must decide how to take care of the absent-other that has been invented by drawing the boundaries of one's own independence. I have offered a reading of an ongoing practice, a phenomenon that is changing, quite literally, as I am writing about it. This, I believe, is one of the challenges and one of the most interesting aspects of studying independent gaming. Suicidal notes such as the one quoted above from Phil Fish, claims of anarchy and political critique such as those pronounced by Molleindustria, and workshops on how to guide oneself and become a successful independent designer, all co-exist as part of the process that constitutes independent gaming. This broad label can be seen as encapsulating a series of ongoing negotiations over the processes of individualisation of various video game producers.

In the next chapter, I will look at the hacking of PlayStation 3 and PlayStation Network. Gamers, hackers, and Sony itself as the publisher of these products have been undertaking a series of contrasting modifications to the PlayStation 3 console and the online gaming service PlayStation Network. These events will be discussed as attempts to claim ownership of a video game, through other means than those of the independent developers. However, at stake there is again the possibility of defining oneself in relation to the technologies used for playing. The hacking of PlayStation Network has been discussed by many commentators in terms of ownership: who really owns a video game console? Who has the right to decide how it can be modified and, ultimately, what it is? As I will argue in the next chapter, there is also a practice of self-definition at play, one that evokes the ethical question of taking care of other players too.

3

They Leak! Hacking PlayStation
(as a) Network

On 4 November 2010, attorney Luanne Sacks was at work at the district court of San Francisco, California. Her role was to defend Sony Computer Entertainment in the litigation that followed the company's decision to remove the OtherOS feature from the PlayStation 3 console. The feature allowed consumers to install any operating system on a PlayStation 3 console. However, many were exploiting this feature to install the Linux operating system and use it to bypass the anti-piracy block and run copied versions of video games. Thus, Sony decided to remove it through a software update of the console, known as firmware 3.21, mandatory for all those who connected to the PlayStation Network (the online gaming platform for Sony's consoles).

When the suspension of OtherOS was announced on 28 March 2010, users expressed their dissatisfaction by posting comments on online forums and on the official PlayStation blog, where the news first appeared. The official release of the firmware was scheduled for 1 April 2010, a date that caused many PlayStation 3 users to think that this was Sony's attempt at an April Fool's joke. This was not the case. The firmware was effectively released as announced, and its consequences were exactly those described by Sony. Even the official PlayStation blog shows the level of disappointment on the part of consumers: the comments on the first announcement unanimously accused Sony of limiting the activity of its users (Seybold 2010). As the protesters argued, installing Linux and connecting several PlayStation 3s in a grid was an economical and effective alternative to buying expensive mainframes. The presence of OtherOS made it possible to use a PlayStation 3 as a computer and therefore extended its potential uses far beyond those strictly related to digital gaming. The new firmware was therefore received by the consumers as a limitation rather than an advancement.

The decision was described by the gaming community as an act of tyranny, an authoritarian decision that threatened their freedom to tinker and play with the technologies they own. The reactions showed feelings of both disillusionment, as Sony was often considered one of the most successful companies in the video game market in terms of attracting and satisfying its customers, and violation of the privacy and rights of the players, who had their data changed or deleted at short notice.[1] Furthermore, the definition that Sony was providing of its own product was seen as arbitrary and old-fashioned. Consumers held that the PlayStation 3 should be deemed a piece of hardware whose functions could be determined and implemented by its users. According to most consumers who complained against Sony's decision, the publisher should not have the authority to determine the legitimate or illegitimate use of the hardware, which should instead be open to player modification. The protests were gathered in a consumer association's complaint, supported by the Electronic Frontier Foundation. In this rapid turn of events, Sony was called, in the person of Luanne Sacks, to defend its right to remove (or add) any feature to the PlayStation 3 and PlayStation Network, while consumers were claiming the right to own what they buy, and not have it forcibly changed by the producer.

Around the time of the California State vs. Sony trial, Sacks was also working as an attorney for Sony in another case, against the hacker George Hotz. Shortly after the release of firmware 3.21, Hotz released a jailbreak to Sony's console, which allowed users to reinstall other operating systems, effectively reintroducing the OtherOS feature. Hotz had declared that the PlayStation 3, as with any other product, is something you own

---

[1] Sony Computer Entertainment was the first video game publisher to release and fully support a game development kit for its own console. Net Yaroze, released in 1997, allowed consumers to produce their own games for the PSone console. While there are previous examples of development kits addressed to indie programmers and hobbyists being released by video game publishers, Net Yaroze was supported by Sony through official competitions and through the Official PlayStation Magazine. Net Yaroze was welcomed by many consumers at the time as an unprecedented opening towards user-produced content.

once purchased, and ownership also implies the right to modify. He had already applied the concept in August 2007, in a famous hack of Apple's iPhone, which unlocked the phone and allowed consumers to use it independently of the original carrier. The two trials became legal contexts in which to decide the freedoms of video game consumers, as well as the definition and boundaries of a video game console.

The events that started in that period generated a series of conflicts that still have repercussions today. The group known as Anonymous decided to take revenge on Sony, which was accused of not respecting its consumers and their freedom to use technologies to their full potential. Anonymous started what is known as Operation Sony, also called OpSony. On 19 April 2011, Sony's servers in San Diego, California, which backed the online service PlayStation Network, reported an anomalous overload. The hacking into the servers forced Sony to suspend PlayStation Network. Officially, Anonymous denied responsibility for this hack. However, the hacking of PlayStation Network took place around the same time as Anonymous announced OpSony. The link between the group and the hack seemed evident to most of the news media that covered this story in the following days. Therefore, in the reconstructions that were publicly released, OpSony and the hacking of PlayStation Network, including the hacking by George Hotz and the following legal debates, all came together to create a unique story.[2] The hacking of online databases and services of other video game publishers in the following days (Codemasters on 10 June, SEGA on 19 June and Bioware on 24 June) seems to confirm that the events surrounding Sony's PlayStation Network were not necessarily related to the release of firmware 3.21 and the deterioration in their relationship with their consumers. More likely, the hacking of PlayStation Network was geared towards stealing sensitive data from users' online transactions. Significantly, the

---

[2] In an article published by Keith Stuart in *The Guardian* (29 April 2011), George Hotz's hacking, Anonymous's OpSony and the hacking of PlayStation Network are distinguished from one other; however, they are analysed as possibly connected events. In the words of Peter Wood of First Base Technologies, the encryption of Sony's firmware is seen as a possible starting point for the more damaging hacking of PlayStation Network. In this version, the events appear separate but also causally linked to one other. However, I note, this does not explain the subsequent hacking of different video game publishers' databases, which were not attacked prior to spring 2011: www.guardian.co.uk/technology/gamesblog/2011/apr/29/psn-hack-industry-reactions (accessed 30 January 2019).

hacking into other publishers' databases received minor media coverage compared to the larger PlayStation 3 case.

The hacking of PlayStation Network became part of a complex narrative that started with the release of firmware 3.21 in April 2010 and culminated with the break-in and the data of 77 million users being stolen. After this rapid series of events, more hacking operations occurred against PlayStation Network. Some of these were claimed as acts of bravado, while others were more likely attempts to steal sensitive data. The latest event occurred in January 2016, when hacker group Fail0verflow, who also took part in the original hacking of PlayStation Network, claimed to have manipulated the PlayStation 4 to let it run games that were not licensed by Sony (in the demonstration of their hack, they showed how a copy of Nintendo's *Pokémon* could run on the console). Sony reacted by shutting down the network until the breach could be fixed, causing anger among their consumers, who could not access a service they had paid for (Martin 2016).

The hacking of Sony's product not only sparked debate about the ownership of the console; more broadly it also prompted a discussion about who has the legitimacy to decide the proper and improper uses of a PlayStation 3, and how consumers and producers can be defined with regard to their rights and duties. The hack was not just about trying to take control of a video game console, it also made claims about what the console could become, and who could manipulate it. It was a direct challenge to Sony that involved the future of the console, and potentially of any digital entertainment product. Furthermore, the debate turned almost immediately on questions around the physical boundaries of the video game console and its online services, since it was not clear to what extent consumer protection law could apply to features, software and parts of Sony's gaming service that are not exactly visible to the eye or physically present in the packaging box. The debate touched on topics such as the temporality of the rights and duties of consumers and producers: for how long can Sony, or the consumers, claim ownership of the console, or how long can the producer be liable for its failures? The questions of the court turned towards an ontology of video game consoles and electronic products: who has the legitimacy to manipulate a PlayStation 3 and PlayStation Network? Is this legitimacy subject to change over time? What exactly are the boundaries of a video game console?

Abstract as they might sound, the questions had immediate conse-quences on the work that attorney Sacks was asked to do. The problem for her, and Sony, was to persuade the court that the one-year warranty that comes with the video game console grants Sony the authority to change any feature of the product after that time period and even not be responsible for its entire malfunctioning. If that warranty was accepted as a legal agreement between Sony and the consumers of its product, then Sony could not be held responsible if only one feature had been changed after four years from the release of the console. In Sacks's own words: 'the only thing that Sony told anyone about the duration of any feature of the PlayStation 3 is what it said in the one year express limited hardware war-ranty. It said one year' (Groklaw 2011).[3]

The details of these events will be discussed throughout the chapter, but it is important to notice that in these accusations and defences, the questions focused on the definition of what can be done with a PlayStation 3 and PlayStation Network, who should be in charge of deciding the legiti-mate uses of the console, and what else these technologies could become. Defining what a video game console *is* and could *become*, through its limits and boundaries in time and space, became the point of debate in a conflict of definitions, in which Sony and its representatives were claiming opposing ideas to those expressed by the consumers of their products.

Ultimately, the debate opened the console itself to unlimited, uncountable forms of hacking – seen here as events that disrupt the appar-ently frozen boundaries of a video game console. These are interruptions that happen in time, and it is within the question of time ('it said one year') that, ultimately, Sony's attorney reclaimed the authority to decide which events, hackings, modifications, and so on could be considered legitimate. The attorney's *intuitive* solution, while acknowledging that technologies and their boundaries change in time, was taken in an authoritative context such as the California district court, where decisions had immediate legal effects and performatively encapsulated the possibilities and constraints offered by the PlayStation 3 and PlayStation Network.

---

[3] The litigations between Sony and consumers, and Sony and the State of California, have been largely reported on Groklaw.net as the events unfolded. In this chapter I refer to the analyses of the trials as they appeared on that website between February and March 2011.

The series of events that became part of what was known as the hacking of PlayStation 3 and PlayStation Network, as happened between 2010 and 2011 (and with numerous repercussions, at least until 2016), has been the source of a multitude of discourses in which the objects – PlayStation 3 and PlayStation Network – have been continuously reframed. In the rest of this chapter, I will refer to the series of events as the *hacking of PlayStation Network*, including in this expression the modifications of the PlayStation 3 console and the other interconnected online services that make the console work and allow players to communicate with each other. As I will argue in this chapter, the notions of *network* and *hacker* are particularly useful when looking at the fluctuating boundaries of Sony's product, as they make us think of this story in terms of relations and transformations rather than objects and definitions.

Conflicting Freedoms

One of the most immediate consequences of the trials has been the emergence of discourses around the definition and duties of producers and consumers of digital entertainment technology. Both sides were arguing about their own possibilities for intervention over PlayStation 3, primarily by posing the question of what a PlayStation 3 is. However, by formulating these questions and demands, they were also defining themselves, their relation to each other and to the video game console. The binary division between producers and consumers was enacted in a variety of contexts, from newspaper articles to public statements and legal trials. The key signifier evoked by most discourses was 'freedom', intended as the freedom to manipulate, modify, own and share. I would like to intervene in the stories surrounding the hacking of PlayStation Network by questioning how divisions between consumers, producers and technological products were brought about, and how the notion of freedom has been used to frame those same divisions.

News media turned their attention towards this story immediately after the hacking of the PlayStation Network in April 2011, during which the sensitive data of 77 million accounts (including credit card information) were illegitimately accessed and saved on a private database. Indeed, the sensationalist terms used by news media in introducing the developments of the case are justified by the vast number of users involved and the significance of a product such as Sony's, which was sold on a global market. The hacking of the PlayStation Network has been described as a breach of an allegedly super-protected and closed environment, which tested consumers' patience and trust (Baker and Finkle 2011; Morris 2011; Carnns 2011; Schiesel 2011). The hacking has indeed had massive consequences, and the reasons are undoubtedly relevant to discourses relating to the ownership of technological products and user privacy. However, I believe that the grounds for interest in this case are quite different from those presented by newspapers and online magazines, as these involve the boundaries of a video game product, the freedom to reshape those boundaries, and the definition of the actors involved in the continuous process of hacking PlayStation Network.

The concept of freedom so often invoked by the hackers, as reported in press releases and public announcements, appears to be inspired by a libertarian ideology, which stresses the role of the individual and his/her potential. According to the hackers of PlayStation Network, consumers should be free to tinker with technology. For instance, hacker George Hotz claims, in an interview on *Wired*, that 'once it's paid for and mine, I have the right to unlock it, smash it, jailbreak it, look at it and hack on it' (Kuchera 2011). In the same period, Hotz also published a video on YouTube where he sings a personal statement in the form of a rap song. In the video, while holding a PlayStation 3 and a printed image of Uncle Sam, he claims to be 'a personification of freedom for all' (Geohot 2011).

Similarly to what Richard Barbrook and Andy Cameron pointed out in 'The Californian Ideology', technology appears in these discourses as a determining force for social change (Barbrook and Cameron 1995). The authors note that this approach to technology began in the 1960s in California and took inspiration from Marshall McLuhan's ideas on media (albeit with several simplifications). According to Barbrook and Cameron, such a view oversimplifies the social and economic complexities of technology, as it puts the individual at the centre of technological development, overshadowing more complex relations of power and the ideological backgrounds to the notion of innovation.

Barbrook and Cameron see in Thomas Jefferson the precursor to the Californian ideology. Jefferson, author of the American Declaration of Independence, thought that private property could constitute a limit to authoritarian governments. If American citizens could each own a piece of land and use it to sustain themselves, then they would be free. Property and ownership could be the foundation of individual freedom. A slave owner and substantial landowner himself, Jefferson's claims regarding freedom appeared to ignore the extent to which this notion of freedom often comes at the cost of restricting the possibilities of others. As Barbrook and Cameron argue, Jeffersonian democracy was intended to be for white people and at the expense of slaves. Similarly, in the hacking of Sony's console, the freedom to manipulate PlayStation 3 and PlayStation Network, according to the statements produced by the hackers and their supporters, comes at the cost of limiting Sony's freedom to change its own product. The ideology espoused by the hackers conceives of freedom as a right of the individual to own their console, and describes its own proposal as purely positive, while it also implies that the original publisher should not control or own developments resulting from their initial product. Moreover, the freedom to manipulate does not necessarily involve the extension of the know-how to include further potential hackers. It is rather oriented to the individual freedom to tinker and manipulate. Sony, on the other hand, claimed freedom to decide what can be included in or excluded from the definition of PlayStation 3 and PlayStation Network, thus limiting the intervention of other parties.

The actors involved in the hacking of PlayStation Network were claiming a specific kind of freedom for themselves, a classical liberal freedom which aims at granting to the individual the liberty *to do* something. Andersson points out that this seems to be a common understanding of the term in the debates in favour of digital piracy:

Along with its countercultural connotations and romantic aura of dissent, 'piracy' here invokes positive liberty: freedom *to* rather than the negative freedom *from*. It is a means to assert one's autonomy, a way of becoming proactive (strategic) rather than reactive (tactical). Piracy here defines the ability to make one's own destiny, to open the black box of technology and utilize it for one's own ends – while doing this in the open, even forming part of the 'mainstream'.

Andersson (2009, 73–4)

The proactive strategies enumerated by Andersson seem to be absent in the hacking of PlayStation Network. As Laura Murray writes while reviewing the movie *Rip! A Remix Manifesto*, claims for a wider freedom are often continuous with 'the base concept of market capitalism, with all its contradictions, rather than a challenge to it' (Murray 2009, 5). Gary Hall has expressed his scepticism about many of the statements produced in favour of digital piracy, stating that 'for all the romantic, counter-cultural associations of its apparent challenge to the commodity culture and property relations of late capitalist society, there is nothing *inherently* emancipatory, oppositional, Leftist, or even politically or culturally progressive about digital piracy' (Hall 2009, 2). After all, the scenario that the hacker George Hotz delineates with his proposition is even more conservative than Sony's. In his attempt to bring back OtherOS and access to those services that were accessible before firmware 3.21 was released, he is not attempting to institute a further system that could possibly include a broader audience, but is re-establishing what already existed.

The Electronic Frontier Foundation supported Hotz by replicating a conception of freedom that implies individualism and ownership. As reported in a public statement released by the foundation:

Sony is sending [a] dangerous message: that it has rights in the computer it sells you even after you buy it, and therefore can decide whether your tinkering with that computer is legal or not. We disagree. Once you buy a computer, it's yours. It shouldn't be a crime for you to access your own computer, regardless of whether Sony or any other company likes what you're doing.

Kushner (2011)

As Hotz declared during an interview on the online video programme *Attack of the Show!*, there is much more at stake in the legal controversy than the destiny of a single man against a corporation, as 'the case is about whether you own that device that you purchased' (Attack of the Show 2011).

Similar statements emerged a few months earlier in different media contexts. The music, movie and book publishing industries have faced similar debates concerning the ownership of digital content. The ability to copy and share digital files undermines the business of most publishers, thus media industries have reacted by implementing forms of control over the digital content they distribute online. Digital rights management (DRM) is one of the most widely adopted anti-piracy technologies for containing the user's control of digital files. Amazon's Kindle, for example, was subject to criticism from consumers and technology reviewers when Amazon deleted a limited number of digital books from Kindle devices without notice, although the consumers were reimbursed. This was seen by many consumers as a breach of their privacy and illegitimate manipulation of an owned device, despite the fact that Amazon explicitly (although not with sufficient transparency) reserved the right to act in similar ways regarding digital copies sold through Kindle (Stone 2009).

As with the hacking of PlayStation Network, the use of DRM in other industries raised debates about the effectiveness of this method in preventing digital piracy and about the limits to consumers' privacy and rights. The fact that the release of digital content through Kindle explicitly referred to the limitations to the ownership of files did not prevent criticism from consumer organisations such as the Electronic Frontier Foundation, who were also very active in defending the hackers of PlayStation Network (Electronic Frontier Foundation 2016). The Kindle case shares some common features with the hacking of Sony's entertainment products, as it also concerns the ownership of both software and hardware. Interestingly, in online forums and news media, both cases have been discussed in relation to freedom, in particular with regard to the meaning of buying a technology and the extent to which this makes the consumer free to have complete access and control over that technology. Jack Schofield, writing in *The Guardian*, describes the Kindle thus:

Although we are used to PCs that offer a wide range of choices at every level, the Kindle is a typical vertically-integrated consumer platform. In these, a single company owns or controls everything (or as much of it as it can) from top to bottom: hardware and software design, content distribution, retailing and sometimes pricing. Apple's iPad and Nintendo's Wii are also examples. Vertically-integrated businesses can develop more integrated products with greater ease of use, while freeing consumers from all the burdens of choice. Basically, you give up your freedom in exchange for a simpler and perhaps more satisfying life.

Schofield (2011)

What are the implications of 'giving up your freedom', and what does it mean to claim it back or demand a more radical sense of control over technological products? The notion of a vertically integrated business does not just have consequences in terms of the number of options and the respective ease of use that a technology can offer. It also reinforces a hierarchical separation between those at the top of such a vertical process and those at the bottom. The story of the hacking of PlayStation Network did not do much to rethink this metaphor of a top-down concession (or privation) of freedom.

The stories that have been narrated, the different versions, perspectives and contexts in which these have been enunciated, all contributed to frame the roles and definitions of the subjects and objects involved, including what is or could be expected from them. Producers and consumers were continuously divided through discourses that assigned them different freedoms. The prolonged controversy between Sony, its consumers and the hackers brought forward opposing notions of what PlayStation 3 (and later PlayStation 4) and the PlayStation Network are and what they should be. Sony, in this process of pushing the boundaries and limits of the PlayStation console, ultimately confirmed its position as the producer and owner of its video game products. Through the statements given in the legal dispute in front of the California State Court, and the press releases produced after the trial, Sony *became* the producer: hierarchically superior, authoritative and therefore distinct from its consumers, Sony received the authorisation for defining what a PlayStation is, while being asked to do so in institutionalised contexts. The statements pronounced in the court performatively defined Sony and assigned to the corporation the role of the producer of PlayStation 3 and PlayStation Network. The same discourses also framed the consumers and their freedoms to modify and play with the video game console.

However, one figure destabilises this dualism between producers and consumers: the *hacker* – a producer and a consumer, a figure with no clear identity, often remaining anonymous, and yet one that modifies the reality surrounding itself. This act of redefinition is a reframing of which nodes, both material and cultural, human (producers and consumers) and non-human (software and hardware) might be included or excluded in PlayStation *as a* network. I will now further explore this notion of the *network*, and consider how hackers become part of it, involving themselves deeply in the technologies they modify and discuss. I believe there is something to be learnt from this practice of involvement, one which incites the hacker to be hospitable towards other hackers and players.

Hybrid Mediators: Becoming Part of the Network

Edge magazine reported a statement by Sony's executive Shinji Hasejima regarding the hacking of PlayStation Network: 'the network vulnerability was a known vulnerability. But Sony was not aware of it . . . was not convinced of it' (Edge 2011, 19). Such a statement speaks to all the meanings of network presented in this chapter. The Sony executive chooses the word to refer to a database of users' data, and possibly also evokes the name of Sony's online service, PlayStation Network. By stating that what is at stake in these events is the hacking of PlayStation *as a* network, I am indeed suggesting a reversal of the meaning of the word. I intend to use it instead as it has been adopted by actor-network theory (ANT) and Bruno Latour (1999, 2005). Considering the involvement of very different elements (social, technological, legal and economic) in the enactment of the definitions of PlayStation Network, I believe Latour's ANT can provide a different perspective on the implications of this case. The vulnerability of the network evoked by Shinji Hasejima might be the defining feature of any network. Networks might in fact be necessarily porous, always leaking and in need of temporary patches.

The dissimilarities between the different uses of the word 'network' suggest that clarifications are needed. Sony's network, the database of information about its users, is allegedly a fixed one. It works by accumulation (the number of registered users is supposed to increase in time) but is mostly a record of information: an archive. Network can also be understood as a point of access to online services (PlayStation Network), but in any case it does not entail transformations of any sort along its nodes. Latour reminds us, instead, to be aware of this new use of the word as it might evoke 'the Internet' and be associated with the idea of information exchange and 'transport without deformation' (Latour 1999, 14). The concept of network he proposed, and the one that I will deploy in relation to viewing PlayStation *as a* network, is composed of plural relations – associations that ceaselessly transform themselves.

As Latour points out when describing ANT, the study of society can be understood both as a study of a state of affairs and as a study of associations. Latour is in favour of the latter, and notices how this type of sociology works particularly well when the participants in the social phenomenon are not 'assembled' yet and are still in a very open process of defining themselves (Latour 2005, 12). This sociology of associations is based on the understanding of the connections as they occur, as they frame themselves, and it is in this sense that I read the events of the hacking of PlayStation Network – not as a social event, structured and ready to be deciphered, but more as an intricate network whose threads can be untangled in innumerable ways and yet reassemble themselves into new shapes every time they are unfolded.

As argued by John Law, entities within a network acquire their attributes because of relations with other entities (Law 1999). ANT is concerned with the displacement, dissolution and fractionality of those relations. Moreover, ANT includes all materials, not only the linguistic side of social phenomena. Networks, Law explains, are composed of linguistic and non-linguistic, human and non-human materials (Law 1999, 3–4). These continuous transformations have some forms of rigidity, which is reached through discursive performativity. For instance, when the Californian State Court lets the attorney Sacks decide the limits of PlayStation Network, she freezes (albeit temporarily and within the context of the trial) the fluidity of all possible associations.

Crucial in this process of change are what Latour calls *mediators*. In the 'sociology of associations' that Latour proposes, mediators can be looked at for the modifications they introduce into a network: 'mediators . . . cannot be counted as just one; they might count for one, for nothing, for several, or for infinity. Their input is never a good predictor of their output; their specificity has to be taken into account every time. Mediators transform, translate, distort, and modify the meaning or the elements they are supposed to carry' (Latour 2005, 39). ANT is about understanding mediators, identifying them and evaluating the changes they introduce. Examples of mediators are, according to Latour, two interlocutors engaged in a conversation, or even a computer that breaks down and generates unpredictable outputs, becoming an agent to understand and decipher.

As Mike Michael argues, ANT has been concerned since its inception with social phenomena in their complex constitution of relations and entities (Michael 2000). ANT, however, leaves us with the question of where the list of entities and relations ends in the constitution of such networks. The list is potentially infinite, and there is some degree of arbitrariness involved in their constitution that allows networks to be understandable as partially closed entities (Michael 2000, 41). What comes to be included and excluded in those networks is the point Michael intends to discuss and present in a different light. He argues: 'a particular human or a human collectivity, a specific technology or a technological system, is the upshot of ongoing configurations of heterogeneous associations' (Michael 2000, 22). The process of establishing a network transforms heterogeneous assemblages of human and non-human entities into collective subjects. To take account of the heterogeneity of a collective subject as it loses its diversity, Michael considers the hybridity of networks and nodes, their co-constitution and the temporary new assemblages that these might constitute.

Michael seeks to invent hybrids, 'that is to say . . . characters made up of a few humans and non-humans (including mundane technologies and aspects of "nature") by which to narrate the processes of ordering and disordering' (2000, 42). Michael then seeks to think of himself as a hybrid, mutually influenced by his own writing, and emerging as a linking entity of 'familiar and novel co(a)gents' (17). It is from these co(a)gents that the writer itself emerges. Mediators can be seen as essentially and necessarily hybrid, and the author of a text, as a source of transformation, can also be regarded as a *hybrid mediator.*

From such a perspective, there are crucial similarities between the hackers and the hybrid mediators that I have introduced through Latour and Michael. Hackers act as hybrid mediators by changing a system and becoming part of it within a single gesture. The hacker as hybrid mediator is both involved within the network and constitutive of it, rather than acting from the outside. Thus, this perspective introduces an intuitive understanding of the act of hacking as it frames the network where it intervenes and, as I will argue, as it happens *in time.*

Conclusion: The Temporality of Networks

In February 2011, the result of the class action started by the consumers' association declared Sony guilty of having violated the Computer Fraud and Abuse Act. Sony's fault was to have advertised OtherOS and then stopped supporting the service. The Sony vs. Hotz trial, instead, was ended by an agreement between the two parties. Sony accused Hotz of helping the piracy industry, while Hotz claimed that his hack was intended to let consumers run their homebrew software and emulators, thus bringing back a greater level of openness into the PlayStation 3 system. As part of the legal settlement, Hotz agreed not to commit any further hacking offences against Sony. In his official statement, he declared: 'it was never my intention to cause any users trouble or to make piracy easier. I'm happy to have the litigation behind me' (Gilbert 2011).

While narrating the story of the hacking of PlayStation Network, I could consider myself to be one more mediator, one more hacker that has disassembled and reassembled a network of nodes. I was, and have always been, a hybrid in the telling of the story of the hacking of PlayStation Network, part of the network I was writing about as much as any other character who has been, or decides to become, a subject in this process of connection and transformation. While the author of the network stays, in Latour's ANT, invisible and detached from the constitution of the network itself, I want to enlarge the network to the point of including its own author. Acknowledging my own presence in this story as hybrid mediator, partly involved in it and partly responsible for its own existence, I offer one further hacking of PlayStation Network in these conclusions.

Who are the consumers and producers of a video game console? Who has the right to decide what can be done with it? Are consumers free to become producers? These questions involve a definition of what a video game console is: what are its boundaries? What can be legitimately done with it? The debate could go on endlessly. Answers to these questions momentarily halt the ongoing series of mediations by including or excluding material and immaterial nodes. However, these pauses can only be *temporary*, which is why I believe that the hacking of PlayStation Network and my role within it must be viewed through a temporal prism.

Definitions of a video game console are *temporary* as they are strategic and *timely*: they outline the uses and limits of a technology and the position to be expected by the actor enunciating such definition. The hackers of PlayStation Network, and Sony itself, have vacillated between different strategic definitions, which have involved themselves and served the purpose of claiming a certain degree of freedom over what they could do with PlayStation 3. Moreover, the temporality of networks can also be understood in a further sense: networks have their own *timing*, as it matters when they are enunciated, and networks are given legitimacy through the position of authority of their mediators. In addition, the cuts that constitute networks reinscribe these *in time*, in a timely progression, delineating what these are before and after the act of mediation.

The hacking of PlayStation Network offers a useful example. The definition of what PlayStation 3, or the PlayStation Network, or any other video game console *is*, is a matter of time: it depends on the timing of the definition itself and its enunciation, which brings about the object of its definition through the very act of its pronouncement. In order to explain this concept I turn to the controversy of the hacking of PlayStation Network and how it was (temporarily) resolved by Sony. Attorney Sacks defended Sony by fixing PlayStation *as a* network by strategically inscribing it within a temporality of her invention: she froze the network in the past (the warranty 'said one year') in order to allow Sony to hack the console in the future and continue to play with it, in its own way. The temporality of this definition was threefold: it was *timely*, as it succeeded in defending Sony; it had its own specific *timing*, as it was pronounced during the trial where the boundaries of the console and the roles of the actors involved were decided institutionally and with legal consequences; finally, it fixed PlayStation Network *in time*, not just providing an abstract definition but one which changes through time, and which understands PlayStation Network in its *becoming something else* (before and after the one-year warranty). In this intervention, attorney Sacks is saying that PlayStation Network is one thing up until one year from its release, and then it can become something else – indeed, here she also implied that Sony had the freedom to decide what else it could then become. Sacks momentarily and intuitively involved herself within the network, only to close it immediately by reaffirming that PlayStation Network only transforms once, at the expiration of the warranty. However, by introducing the notion of time within the definition of a video game console, she also complicated its boundaries. It might become impossible to say what a video game console is, if its limits are drawn by speakers who are hybrid mediators, involved in the same time and space of the technological product, and transforming themselves as they define the console and play with it.

The resolution of the California State Court is only one of many instances of the hacking of Sony's products. A multitude of hackers has introduced the notion that video game consoles can be breached: consoles leak, and their drops evaporate, occupying as much space as the environment allows; video game consoles are porous, malleable, liquid or even gaseous things. What is sold in the packaging box is unpredictable and changes in time. The box in which the console is packed is one more mediator in the network, which poses a temporary physical boundary to the console, before its solidity sublimates. Once opened, the console is unboxed, flexible and plastic. The components of a video game console are altered, consumed and used in diverse ways. Consoles are altered by their manufacturers through updates and patches, and the roles of those who control these alterations, and those who make the console and then play with it (or make it *as* they play with it), change accordingly. Sometimes these changes prove to be conflictual with other players, while at other times they are hospitable and welcoming. It is not just consoles with online connections that show their necessary malleability and constant leaking; hardware in general is always under erosion. After all, hacking has a longer history than the Internet, although video game consoles that require an online connection surely offer greater resonance to shared acts of manipulation.

The temporality of the network can be disturbed. The hacker, as a hybrid mediator, can establish different networks. Reconfiguring existing games via software and hardware modifications, opening the black boxes of technologies, could become a way of exploring channels of communication between a multitude of nodes and escaping the binaries underpinning oppositional discourses between producers and consumers. Becoming hybrid mediators also requires acknowledging that gamers and scholars are inevitably implicated in the technologies they discuss, and that they participate in their definition – as I am doing *now*, as I write. Being involved to such an extent also entails agreement to take care of all the others involved in the same network, thus avoiding libertarian, individualistic and oppressive perspectives. Video game consoles can be hacked while playing with them, but the interpretation given to one's freedom within the network can make the difference between being a good or a bad hacker.

These conclusions could also be seen as an elaboration of Wendy Chun's argument that networks and mediators, in the understanding provided by Bruno Latour and ANT, seem to have become an easy answer that simplifies social interactions by reducing them to nodes and connections (Chun 2016). Chun argues that in the current neoliberal environment, individuals become more frequently separated from each other, and as such, understanding the formation of collectivities as momentary connections between distant nodes risks providing a simple solution, one that shuts down further questioning and inquiry, and in fact reinforces the 'emergence, management, and imaginary of neoliberalism' (2016, 16). The connections between nodes, Chun points out, are imagined spatialisations of time, of repeated actions and exchanges of information. The lines connecting dots in a network are habits, frequently repeated actions devoid of any meaning in themselves but mediating, or transforming, the network itself and its nodes. My proposal is that, by thinking of my own involvement in the network as a hybrid mediator, the action of writing and talking about the network becomes a transformative event rather than a habit. The different timing of the academic intervention (a concept I further explore in the conclusions of this book), as well as Sacks' speech at the California State Court, or the acts of the hackers who modify PlayStation Network, disrupt the cycles of habit and introduce new temporary connections. These are not just mediations to look at and draw on a map of edges, nodes and lines; rather, they are performances that occur at the boundaries of the network, altering its limits, and inaugurating a period of crisis.

The stories of the hacking of PlayStation Network show that video games, in both software and hardware, are malleable entities that can only temporarily be defined and strategically framed as part of a network. These networks and definitions involve the speaker, the actor who puts the video game *back in a box*. Not all definitions are the same, though, and those provided by Sony's attorney matter more than the others because they are granted legitimacy and authority by the place in which they are enunciated. Defining video games is a matter of power: the technical aspects, the uses and audiences, the rights and duties of producers and consumers and even their own definition can only be defined as the result of institutionalised speech acts – such as those produced in academic publications, for instance. These acts invent the time of the process of mediation, deciding when and how technologies transform and translate.

This has been my personal intervention in the crisis of PlayStation Network: I have involved myself in it, becoming part of the problem rather than the solution. My proposal consists in an alternative narrative of the hacking. The hacking has not fixed the roles of producers and consumers, nor has it established the limits of digital entertainment products. Instead, it has revealed their porosity, and how they change in time. I have proposed that Sony's attorney responded intuitively to the question of defining what a video game console is and could be, by introducing duration and time as part of the solution. However, she also exposed that the speaker is part of the problem, being *anxiously at stake in the game*. Thus, it matters who the speaker is, when and where the network is frozen, and for what purposes. In this chapter, I have performed a further hacking of the network, in my own time, by writing about it and reframing its flexible nodes, and utilising, like hackers before me, my individual freedom to tinker with what I (do not) own.

In the next chapter, I will explore another example of a video game that has been transforming itself over a prolonged period of time, and where the reconstruction of the temporality of its transformations is even more problematic. This is a video game that was buried in a desert in New Mexico and, from that moment on, it became uncontainable to an extent that could not have been predicted. Its invisibility underground had the opposite effect of putting it under the spotlight of the histories of the medium. I am referring to the story of the video game *E.T. the Extra-Terrestrial*, a commercially unsuccessful product which Atari, its producer, decided to discard by disposing of its cartridges. *E.T.* is a significant case to discuss the ways in which the history of the medium is told and how this again implies the time and timing of its enunciation in deeply destabilising ways, to the point that the present itself becomes unstable. To know more about this story it is not necessary to dig too deep, or to get one's hands dirty with mud. All that is required is to move to the next chapter and get ready to challenge an oxymoron: that an extra-terrestrial could be buried underground.

4

A History of Boxes: Game Archaeology and the Burial of *E.T. the Extra-Terrestrial*

The First Video Game Ever

In the previous chapter I discussed how the boxing of video games, which transforms them into products with defined boundaries, raises questions about the authority of the voices that produce the definitions of digital games and determine their material and immaterial limits. Definitions are often contested through debates about how alternative boxes could be imagined and produced: for example, by proposing other understandings and uses of video game software and consoles; by asking who owns them and for how long these boxes should hold; and by questioning whether they should be kept always open and malleable.

While the case of the hacking of PlayStation 3 and the PlayStation Network raises these issues explicitly, there are other circumstances where similar authoritarian acts regulate the limits and possibilities of the medium of the video game in less explicit terms. The historiographies of the medium are another area in which video games are defined in relation to their uses, influences and cultural relevance while being seen in their historical progression. As argued in the introduction, narratives about the past, present and future of video games often imagine a progressive development of technological products. The problem of determining the very first video game ever made is a perfect example of the ontological controversy underlying these historical projects: how can anyone decide which of the first playful experiments with a digital technology truly qualifies as a video game? What is the key property that transforms a digital text into a video game?

The stories of *Tennis for Two* (1958) and *Spacewar* (1962) are excellent examples. Reconstructions of the history of video games generally agree on designating 1958 as year one of electronic gaming, when William Higinbotham, while working at the Brookhaven National Laboratory in Upton, New York, used an oscilloscope to design a game called *Tennis for Two* with a view to entertaining students who were visiting the research centre. A few years later, in 1962, at the Massachusetts Institute of Technology (MIT), Stephen Russell designed *Spacewar*. The game required two players and was a simulation of a fight between two spaceships. Higinbotham's *Tennis for Two* was addressed directly to students and visitors, and was not advertised anywhere other than the Brookhaven National Laboratory. *Spacewar* was conceived explicitly as software to be shared among researchers with access to one of the first computer models, the PDP-1 (Programmed Data Processor-1).

Steven Poole acknowledges *Spacewar* to be the first video game ever made, as does John Anderson in an article published in *Creative Computing Video and Arcade Games* in Spring 1983 (Poole 2000, 15; Anderson 1983). Jessie Herz, in one of the first texts to present video game culture to a wider audience, ignores *Tennis for Two* and places the beginning of the medium of the video game with the invention of *Spacewar* (Herz 1997). Steven L. Kent, while acknowledging *Tennis for Two* as the first video game, claims that it was an isolated case that did not influence Stephen Russell, who should be regarded, according to Kent, as one of the real inventors of digital gaming (Kent 2001, 18).

The difficulty of deciding which one is the first lies in the conditions in which these experiments were produced and played at the time. In both cases there was no sense of a finished product. *Spacewar* has been described by many accounts of the history of computer hacking as one of the first examples of an always-open piece of coding, continuously modified by different engineers across the (few) research laboratories in the United States that had access to a PDP-1 (Levy 2010, 39–60). In contrast, *Tennis for Two* could be played in only one specific place, and did not have the characteristics of a sharable or mass-produced digital product like video games are today. It is impossible to decide the final configuration of the software that made both games. In fact, even the word software still had to be invented, as coding was not seen as something that could possibly be framed as a finished text.

What were *Tennis for Two* and *Spacewar*, then? If not clearly identifiable entities but a series of operations and attempts to play with the earliest computers, how did they come to be defined as the first video games ever, or as two among the very first? In Jeffrey Fleming's 'Down the Hyper-Spatial Tube: *Spacewar* and the Birth of Digital Game Culture', one of the co-authors of *Spacewar*, J. G. Graetz, remembers the days when the game was in (permanent) development (Fleming 2007). When asked about his feelings when a similar game was released, fifteen years later, as a coin-operated machine by a video game company (*Space Wars* by Larry Rosenthal in 1977), he acknowledges that the idea of copyrighting *Spacewar* crossed their minds, but they did not consider the full implications:

Nobody knew what programming was. It was something you did to make a computer do things but it had no existence apart from the computer. . . . The word 'software' didn't come into existence until just about the time that we got Spacewar done. In fact, the first use of the word in a DEC catalog spelled it wrong. Even after it had a name, nobody knew what it was.

Fleming (2007, 4)

As also argued by Nathan Ensmenger, in the history of computing, the separation between software and hardware, as well as the emergence of the figure of the programmer, appears separately and later in respect of computers as a technology (Ensmenger 2010).

How could these ineffable things that were made in the late 1950s and 1960s come to be identified, more than thirty years later, as the first representatives of a new medium? I believe this has happened mostly because the history of the medium of the video game has appeared as the history of an industry, and of its progressive (and often unquestioned) economic success. As such, the history of video games has so far been seen as the history of a series of commercial products and of their consumers. The lack of an identifiable unity, a packaged and closed product, has been problematic for the stories surrounding the emergence of *Tennis for Two* and *Spacewar*. The multiple and uncountable forms of these two games could not be taken into account by a historical endeavour into the origins of the video game which took the existence of an industry as paramount for the formulation of a historical project.

By framing the history of video games as an industry, retrospective studies have tended to look for those unities and products that the industry itself was producing. In so doing, the history of video games has often been a history of boxes, and boxes have been seen, and found, even when these could not possibly exist, as in the case of *Tennis for Two* and *Spacewar*.

With this metaphor of the box, I intend to unsettle the reassuring visions that histories of gaming have replicated so far. As Joost Van Loon argues, media cannot be understood without taking into consideration their historicity, the historical context in which they come into being. This not only works 'as an antidote to modes of thinking that attempt to read the "essence" of a medium purely from its internal, technological properties', but is also a methodological prerequisite for understanding media and their evolution through the cultural context in which they have been developed and used (Van Loon 2008, 12). This is what Van Loon calls the cultural embedding of a technology: 'culture highlights that meaning and significance emerge from practices and do not exist in themselves' (2008, 13). The telling of the history of video games to date has been primarily *disembedded* from the contexts in which the events of those histories occurred. Video games are seen as things that just happened, that appeared in the timeline of technological progress of our culture, rarely taking into account the processes of connection and transformation (or remediations, as Bolter and Grusin put it; see Bolter and Grusin 1999) between diverse experiences and understandings of digital technologies. Moreover, such an approach to the history of the medium is disembedded from the present, from the time and place of its enunciation, which implicitly appears as homogeneous and fixed.

However, in these historical accounts which look chronologically at the appearance of boxes, there must surely be some false steps, discrepancies or inconsistent trajectories that do not make immediate sense, or that represent plain failures in the otherwise splendid growth of the video game industry. In this chapter, I will take one specific example of a failure in the history of the video game industry. It is the story of *E.T. the Extra-Terrestrial*, a video game developed and published by Atari in 1982, the copies of which were discarded soon after by the company in an attempt to save on the storage costs of the unsold cartridges. The product was a disaster in economic terms, as sales were much lower than expected.

The story of *E.T.* is interesting for at least two reasons. First, it is literally the story of a collection of boxes: accounts, official and unofficial, talk of thousands of cartridges of the video game being buried in the desert of New Mexico. Like the stories of *Tennis for Two* and *Spacewar*, game historians have been trying to find these boxes, reconstructing their presence through documents and, in the case of *E.T.*, digging in the desert to find evidence of their existence. Such an obsession over the boxes of video games has also been justified through the coinage of a new term and profession, namely, the *video game archaeologist*. Media archaeology is also the name given to the study of the history of media, and the relation between the field of academic research and the physical burial of *E.T.* will be explored in the rest of this chapter.

Secondly, the story of the video game *E.T.* is a fitting example to discuss the excessive confidence that pervades the historical reconstructions of the medium of the video game, particularly when these are used to reflect on the present time and context in which they are written. Allegedly, the story of *E.T.* is regarded as a curiosity and an example of how digital gaming has gone through major economic crises before becoming the most important sector in the globalised entertainment industry. The crisis of 1982–85 is considered one of the most significant interruptions in the otherwise continuous development of the video game industry, mostly caused by a saturated market of clone products (Wolf 2012). Eventually, after 1985, the video game industry moved to Japan and Nintendo became, at that time, the most important producer of consoles and games. Atari played a major role in this market crash as the leader of the industry in the early 1980s. Atari's consoles were saturated with video game products made by Atari and third-party companies, but very few of these products were of a reasonably good quality. The story of *E.T.* marks the epitome of this abundance of unwanted products that led to a significant pause in the economic growth of the sector and the rise of Japan as the leading market.

The crash of 1982–85, of which the burial of *E.T.* is symbolic, sheds light on the frictionless relationship that most of the written histories of the video game have with their own past and with the present. The past is often seen as a series of events to be looked at while unfolding, and which lead to the present, seen as a stable and safe destination point. But what is the significance of the interruptions and crashes in the historical progression of the medium? By what criteria are exceptions identified and understood as such? In whose history is *E.T.* appearing as a collection of unsold and unwanted boxes? These questions are not usually considered in the historical and archaeological approaches to video games, and I believe this is the result of an inflated confidence in the stability of the present, seen as a fixed state of practices of production and consumption, which can be transparently analysed and understood. The excavation of *E.T.* is in fact quite controversial in this sense, and its implications will be discussed in the next section.

The Afterlife of *E.T. the Extra-Terrestrial*

On 26 April 2014, Microsoft spokesman Larry Hryb announced via Twitter that the expedition to find the buried cartridges of the 1982 video game *E.T. the Extra-Terrestrial* had been successful. The story of the game attained the status of urban legend in video game culture. As reported in many texts about the history of the medium, Atari developed the video game *E.T.* after a highly anticipated deal with film producer Universal Pictures, which gave Atari the rights to release video games based on the successful film directed by Steven Spielberg. However, the game turned out to be very disappointing, and it was released at a time (the early 1980s) when the video game industry was struggling to sell enough to maintain itself. As the legend goes, Atari decided to eliminate the unsold cartridges by burying them in the desert near Alamogordo, New Mexico. In 2014, Microsoft and the film company Fuel Industries obtained the rights to excavate the area to try to find proof of this legend as part of a documentary project on video games.

One of the cartridges found in the desert has been donated to the Smithsonian Museum of American History. On their website, museum specialist Drew Robarge announces the addition to the collection in grandiloquent tone:

The cartridge is one of the defining artifacts of the crash and of the era. In addition to the crash, the cartridge can tell many stories: the ongoing challenge of making a good film to a video game adaptation, the decline of Atari, the end of an era for video game manufacturing, and the video game cartridge life cycle. The cartridge also serves as closure for many things: the urban legend of the burial, the golden years of Atari, an era where American companies dominated the console scene. All of these possible interpretations make for a rich and complicated object. As they say, one man's trash is another man's treasure.

Robarge (2014)

The story of the discovery of Atari's dumped cartridges, as related by Microsoft and other press sources, can be taken as an example of how histories of the medium of the video game often tend to operate. In fact, the excavation was attempting to discover evidence of a story already written and repeated in several (more or less official) contexts in which the events around the game company Atari were analysed. The archaeological endeavour aimed at providing proof of something that was already expected to be true – namely, that copies of the game *E.T.* had been buried in the desert. The contemporary knowledge about the story of Atari was seen as the point of destination, as the safe arrival of the archaeological research.

In *Game After: A Cultural Study of Video Game Afterlife*, Raiford Guins approaches the story of *E.T.* from what he defines as an archaeological perspective (Guins 2014). In his text, this means looking at the documents and remains of *E.T.* in a very detailed analysis of the first-hand accounts of residents of Alamogordo, New Mexico, searching the coordinates of where the game boxes were buried and the articles and interviews about the story of Atari and the development of the game. In Guins' work there is a strong focus on experiencing, in the first person, the stories that make video game culture, by witnessing, seeing and hearing what video game collectors, designers and hobbyists have to say and getting in touch with what is left of old coin-operated machines and video game consoles. Objects and things, Guins argues, have an afterlife: after their disposal they continue to exist as collectables or in museum archives, and in some cases, as happened with *E.T.*, as trash. Yet this is trash that continues to inspire stories and events, such as the excavation that recently took place in New Mexico.

Drawing on the work of Don Ihde, Guins argues that objects are 'multistable', as they can be 'many things at once' (Guins 2014, 12). From this, Guins proposes that in the analysis of video games, and artefacts in general, it should be asked not only what something is but also when and where it is, how it emerges and how it is used. This would amount to taking into consideration its afterlife. In Guins' analysis of *E.T.* there is great consideration of how the game was originally perceived by journalists and critics, as well as how it is now perceived in gamers' communities, how the packaging was made and what sort of economic conditions caused Atari to suffer such a commercial disaster.

Guins is effective in illustrating the stories surrounding the video game *E.T.*; however, his approach to what this game *is* too easily evades the problems deriving from the ontological questions he formulates. The solution Guins finds, as in many other media archaeological accounts, is in the *context*: *E.T.* needs to be explained through the context in which it was conceived, produced, played, trashed and excavated. His definition of archaeology is to 'look around things' in order to understand them (Guins 2014, 7). Archaeology therefore remains a form of truth seeking, and the problem of defining the conditions for seeking and saying the truth about video games ultimately relies on the context in which these truths allegedly appear to the archaeologist (Guins 2014, 234).

Thus, the context is presented as a larger and safer container for a rather unstable and *leaking* reality (as I already argued in relation to the hacking of PlayStation Network). However, as Jaakko Suominen effectively argues, there are 'many ways to contextualize' the history of gaming (Suominen 2016, 6). Suominen classifies four different methods of contextualising history across hundreds of publications on the medium of the video game published since 2002. The 'enthusiastic' accounts, written for gamers and people who are passionate about the medium, tend to present a rather linear narrative of progress. The 'emancipatory' studies seek instead to establish alternative histories and highlight marginal characters and events in video game culture. The 'genealogical' approaches, which include the work of Raiford Guins, operate more like scientifically rigorous antiquaries and often discuss the medium through biological metaphors (using expressions such as 'the evolution of the medium'), Suominen argues. Finally, the 'pathological' studies of the history of video games refer directly to Foucault's notion of archaeology and are 'most generally focused on the pre- and protohistories of games, [and tend] to underline ruptures, anomalies, material, embodied, and experiential as well as experimental aspects of contemporary game cultures' (Suominen 2016, 12). These studies present themselves as 'deep excavations', often focused on early and dismissed technologies. The pathological accounts have often looked at specific consoles, defining the study known as 'platform studies' (Montfort and Bogost 2009). The arbitrariness of studies on specific game platforms has been contested (Apperley and Parikka 2015). Suominen argues that at the foundation of pathological approaches there is the same kind of search for a revelation, a hidden truth: '(most of) the media archaeology and platform studies share a distinct pathological view: both are interested in an artifact's "inner life," opening the black box – or a postmortem of a corpse – with divergent tools' (2016, 13).

My argument is that, with the exception of some of the studies that Suominen labels as emancipatory, these different forms of study and contextualisation of the past have a problem with how they relate to the present. The image of archaeological digging – so often evoked by studies into the history of gaming – is particularly emblematic of this problem, as it hides the ground on which the excavation is carried out. In the case of *E.T.*, its afterlife has yet to be seen as a new form of life that could haunt the present, but is rather seen as a congealed life, put on display and discussed from a safe distance. The extra-terrestrial found by the archaeological expedition has been described as if it were a mummy: rigid and perfectly preserved. However, as I will now argue, it could also be seen as a ghost: floating and ineffable.

Media Archaeology and the Problem of the Present

As argued by Erkki Huhtamo and Jussi Parikka, the field of media archaeology has been based on two different readings of Foucault's understanding of the term *archaeology* (Huhtamo and Parikka 2011). On the one hand, one reading has been inspired by Marshall McLuhan and has moved in the direction applied by Friedrich Kittler. This perspective emphasises the role of technology in the production of knowledge. On the other hand, the Anglo-American tradition tends to assume that technologies are introduced within a pre-existing discursive context which frames the uses and interpretations of the technology (Huhtamo and Parikka 2011, 8–15). In many cases, as in those presented in the collection of essays edited by

Huhtamo and Parikka, the interplay between technologies and discourses is placed at the centre of the analysis.

I argue that what consistently appears in those archaeological accounts, whichever reading of Foucault is applied, is the possibility of explaining how certain phenomena happened, how they transformed themselves, and the rules under which these changes occurred. Technologies and discourses are seen as mutating through a series of conditions that have to be discovered. Media archaeology abounds with metaphors that evoke a physical excavation, a process of revelation that is made possible by digging, vertically, deep into the historical documents. Erkki Huhtamo, one of the most prolific media archaeologists to also look at the medium of the video game, describes this approach towards the past in quite explicit terms. In 'Slots of Fun, Slots of Trouble: An Archaeology of Arcade Gaming', Huhtamo argues that 'electronic games did not appear out of nowhere; they have a cultural background that needs to be excavated' (Huhtamo 2005, 4). In the same text, the appearance of early video games in public spaces (arcade gaming) is described in relation to similar interfaces where touching and finger movements were also used for entertainment purposes. Huhtamo affirms that these 'devices provided the ground for future applications such as electronic arcade games'; however, 'how, why, when and where this happened is a challenge for scholars', therefore 'what is needed is an "archaeology of gaming"' (ibid.).

However, there is no further argument for the need for such archaeology. I propose that the need is mostly motivated by the wish to explain how, why, when and where something happened. It is an explanatory endeavour, one that believes in observation and analysis as objective approaches (although these are named excavations). In the conclusions of the same paper, Huhtamo maintains that 'excavating the past makes sense when trying to explain phenomena like arcade video gaming with seemingly very short histories' (2005, 15). According to Huhtamo, the list of technologies to connect in order to explain the current scenario includes kinetoscopes and mutoscopes, slot machines and flippers, and all machines that require physical actions to be activated and played with. The excavation appears to be a detailed narrative of historical progression, which has 'continuity and rupture, similarity and difference, tradition and innovation' (2005,

5) but still allows us to trace one evident and single narrative out of the many marginal ones.

Jussi Parikka and Jaakko Suominen, in 'Victorian Snakes? Towards a Cultural History of Mobile Games and the Experience of Movement', debate the origins of mobile gaming through a similarly defined archaeological approach (Parikka and Suominen 2006). The aim of the paper is to draw on media archaeology and history to explain the emergence of the use of mobile devices for digital play. The authors argue that while historiographies of video games have looked too closely and exclusively at the events surrounding the game industry, their paper attempts instead to broaden the perspective to include documents, events, and technologies from other areas that could have contributed to contemporary mobile gaming. The history of the forms of entertainment used while travelling and commuting, from printed books to the Sony Walkman, positions mobile gaming among a more varied series of commodities and considers it dependent upon changing social habits and work conditions in which transportation is used more frequently.

The title of the paper 'Victorian Snakes' refers to the main question posed by the author. Inspired by the work of Tom Standage, who, in *The Victorian Internet*, compares the telegraph to a contemporary Internet of the Victorian age, the authors aim to find a Victorian *Snake* (a hugely popular mobile video game by Nokia first introduced in the company's mobile phones in 1997) (Standage 1999). Parikka and Suominen propose to 'steer clear of such easily anachronistic comparisons between times and technologies', but still ask 'in which sense can we claim the existence of a Victorian equivalent of Snake or of other mobile games? That is, in what sense are mobile games part of a longer duration of modern experience and media consumption?' (Parikka and Suominen 2006, 7).

In the introduction to this book, I referred to the work of Derrida and his re-evaluation of the anxiety that results from being 'implicated in the game, of being caught by the game, of being as it were from the very beginning at stake in the game' (Derrida 1980, 248). What Huhtamo, Parikka and Suominen are instead offering appears to be a very confident approach to the study of digital games, and media in general. Even if each of them acknowledges the possibility of different historical narratives and the partiality of his own views, they maintain that looking at the past in a linear, teleological and progressive manner could contribute to the understanding of the present. However, what results from these narratives is the exclusion of the present as the moment from which the past is looked at, narrated, and in fact constructed. The present, from where the authors analyse and excavate the past, appears as a safe destination point.

From Archaeology to Genealogy

Game archaeology shares with media archaeology the confidence that results from accepting that the present can be explained through the past, even if explanations are to remain temporary and provisional. The explanation of the present through the past is also the main and only rationale for such archaeological studies. As Jussi Parikka explains:

> A lot of media-archaeologically tuned research has been in writing counter-histories to the mainstream media history, and looking for an alternative way to understand how we came to the media cultural situation of our current digital world. It is for media archaeologists as it was for Foucault: all archaeological excavations into the past are meant to elaborate our current situation.
>
> Parikka (2012, 6)

My concern is precisely with the 'current situation' and its relevance in archaeological studies. Rephrasing Michel Foucault, Parikka and Suominen propose that '(cultural) archaeology can be defined as the unconscious level of a culture that enables the actual perceived forms of everyday life. The archaeological level enables the objects, ideas, thoughts, experiences, etc. of a certain historical situation' (Parikka and Suominen 2006, 9).

My critique of game archaeology does not intend to question the accuracy of those descriptions, but rather it is mostly concerned with the stabilising effect that these have on the perception of the contemporary situation. Michel Foucault's original project of an archaeology of knowledge was not necessarily intended as an elaboration of the present through the past but as an inquiry into the fragility of any system of thought, including our own, when confronted with its genealogy. The turn to genealogy in Foucault's work is quickly dismissed by Parikka, as he acknowledges that in genealogy 'the emphasis was more on questions of "descent" and critique of origins as found in historical analysis of his time', which were the foundation for Foucault's counter-histories (Parikka 2012, 6). But genealogy, as Foucault puts it, was not about finding the origins of an event in order to restore its apparent unity. On the contrary, genealogy aims to:

Maintain passing events in their proper dispersion; it is to identify the accidents, the minute deviations – or conversely, the complete reversals – the errors, the false appraisals, and the faulty calculations that gave birth to those things that continue to exist and have value for us; it is to discover that truth or being does not lie at the root of what we know and what we are, but the exteriority of accidents.

Foucault (1991, 81)

In Foucault's *History of Sexuality*, the main problem is not simply tracing how differences and truths were affirmed, in different periods of history, in relation to sexuality. It is not about finding out the equivalent of sexuality in the Victorian age, as in Standage's search for a Victorian Internet or Parikka and Suominen's Victorian Snake. Foucault's research is about the present, and the conditions for saying the truth about sexuality in our age. The Victorian age and other historical eras are examined so as to discover the contingencies that have determined the current conditions for differentiating between truth and falsehood with regard to a specific notion (of which sexuality could be an example). How does truth come to be constructed as such, and could it not be otherwise? Foucault does not attempt to colonise the past with the questions of the present, but rather aims to challenge the notions of the present by tracing their genealogy. In Foucault's work, 'the history of the present designates precisely the point where historical reflection and a critical attitude from within and towards the present articulate the production of a difference within history' (Tazzioli, Fuggle and Lanci 2015, 2).

Conclusion: I Want to Believe

As soon as the first pictures of the retrieval of *E.T.* appeared online, gamers and video game collectors started speculating about the evidence that was provided. As reported on *Ars Technica*, an online magazine about technology and culture, many interruptions had postponed the moment when the cartridges were revealed. The website states that the first two excavations, to which selected journalists and a number of interested fans had been invited, were unsuccessful. Initially, some of the pits were inaccessible. Later, other excavations produced no results. Only after the first two attempts were press and fans invited to a third excavation. This last attempt quickly revealed a copy of *E.T.*, buried quite superficially in the desert. Moreover, only one copy of the game was shown, and a few other Atari products appeared in the photos of the excavated area. Speculation arose that the mission had, in fact, failed to produce results, and the photo and video evidence found was actually planted in the pits overnight by the documentary film-makers. Kyle Orland from *Ars Technica* comments:

The simple fact that the film crew found some cartridges seems unlikely to fully kill the legend. Even today, new conspiracy theories are popping up to replace the old. Some Internet trolls are already suggesting that the Microsoft-affiliated film crew planted the cartridges for the benefit of the cameras and that the media has either been snookered or is in on it. Yesterday's dig did debunk some of those 'I heard . . .' myths (there were some games down there besides *E.T.*, for instance), but it left others frustratingly unaddressed (archaeologist Andrew Reinhard told *Ars* 'there's no way' to estimate how many games were buried).

Orland (2014)

Through the speculation and rumours that circulated in online communities and video game magazines, the *E.T.* cartridges lost their apparent solidity. When confronted with the multiple narratives that make sense of their presence, solid objects tend to evaporate. Materiality had been used as evidence in the story of *E.T.*, but what made the cartridges and the photos of them relevant *as evidence* was mostly a discursive construction, a series of narratives told and repeated in books, online forums and the press releases from the documentary film-makers. The evidence was revealed to be relevant because of, and for, the words and the meanings associated with it in a specific community. Those same words can be said to be the very event that constituted the rediscovery of *E.T.*: the discourses generated by the archaeologists and gamer communities motivated the generation of further discourses about the discovery of *E.T.* and its later rebuttal. Those words had always been material, tangible and productive of visible effects.

As long as the question is one of revealing the truthfulness of the story of Atari's *E.T.*, there can always be alternative stories to tell. *E.T.* is important and relevant to us as a story, and as such it is probably more interesting to inquire into these stories and discuss the conditions for telling the truth about Atari's *E.T.*, and what is at stake in inventing other stories (even ones that need not be true). Through discourse, narratives are replicated, and the material evidence, the excavations and mud, the boxes that make and contain video games are framed and remediated. Archaeologists, filmmakers, fans and gamers have been involved in shaping multiple narratives of *E.T.*, and finding the cartridges is a part of those narratives. In the same way, I am (as gamer, academic and author of this chapter) partly responsible for determining what constitutes the objectivity of the history of games. I am and have always been involved in deciding why, how, and to whom the history of *E.T.* is relevant.

The problem has never been what *E.T.* is and where it is, but how it becomes what it is, and what else it could be. The articles in *Ars Technica* phrase this problem well by asking: 'Why are we so interested in some buried hunks of plastic and silicon?' Taken as a non-rhetorical question, this exposes the problem of understanding the reason why these stories are told. The question introduces the problem of the present, seen as an unstable position from which to view the past.

Michel Foucault maintained exactly this in his consideration of the unities of history: 'I shall accept the groupings that history suggests only to subject them at once to interrogation; to break them up and then to see whether they can be legitimately reformed; or whether other groupings should be made' (1972, 29). The responsibility of searching for other unities is what makes telling history a form of intervention; it is what makes it responsibly and ethically performative. The instability that results from this other archaeology is something that needs to be taken care of.

Michel Serres proposed that historical eras, as well as objects, can be seen as multifaceted and as continuously folding into different unities: 'every historical era is likewise multitemporal, simultaneously drawing from the obsolete, the contemporary, and the futuristic. An object, a circumstance, is thus polychromic, multitemporal, and reveals a time that is gathered together, with multiple pleats' (Serres and Latour 1995, 60). From this perspective, an archaeological view cannot take the present for granted as this becomes the result of a discursive, temporary and strategic folding. The present time in the archaeological perspective is a unity captured through discourse while in its undoing.

My intervention in this chapter has consisted in joining (and enjoying) this undoing. I have been writing a different narrative of *E.T.*, investigating its relevance in the historical reconstructions of the medium, and questioning the authorities that preside over its relevance. What are the conditions for saying the truth about video games, as well as their past, present and future? The history of video games can be approached to reaffirm our present knowledges about the medium, or it can be seen, more *creatively*, as the result of a series of performances. Statements such as those presented in written publications on the history of video games, press releases and articles by game scholars, gamers, journalists, and even the act of burying copies of *E.T.* in the desert, uncovering those copies and displaying them in a museum, taking photographs and publishing them as proofs: all such acts are performances that rewrite history, undoing it and reassembling its nodes. My act of writing about *E.T.* is another performative event, and as such it is anxiously involved in history and its undoing: it is a new writing of history, another narrative (and part) of the past, present and future of video games.

What is at stake, then, when considering our own involvement in the construction of a history of gaming? What are the consequences of being part of the game? In the next chapter I will discuss some recent events where the description of a historical change in the consumer base of video game products has been used to justify a series of misogynist attacks against the presence of women in video game culture. The series of events, known as GamerGate, involved the telling of a history of the medium, one in which male gamers formed the original producers and consumers to be replaced, only recently, by more varied categories of consumers, most notably women. GamerGate has generated several different narratives of how women (and, as I will discuss, academia and the game industry) were attempting to take control of the medium and shape its present and future. Many of the aggressive and conspiratorial stories that circulated under the umbrella of the GamerGate campaign were questioning, and claiming for themselves, the authority to dictate the history of the medium: to whom do video games belong? And who has the authority to answer this question? As I will argue, the events surrounding GamerGate prompt us to reconsider our own presence in the formulation of these (unresolvable) questions.

5

GamerGate: Becoming Parasites to Gaming

Linus: Remember, it rains on the just and the unjust
Snoopy: But why us in-betweens?

Peanuts, by Charles M. Schulz, 13 April 2004

Since August 2014, the representation of women in games and their inclusion in the games industry have been at the centre of heated debates within video game culture. The debates are the outcome of a series of verbal and written accusations made against women, who are seen by a large group of male gamers as a threatening force, intruding into the traditional gaming audience to disrupt the medium and influence the production of video games by imposing gender equality and fair representation. The attacks on women have mostly taken place online, but real-life threats have also been made against those women who became publicly notorious for questioning how gender is represented in video games and within games culture. The harassment campaign against women took the name *GamerGate*. GamerGate is in fact a word, or Twitter hashtag, used to identify a much broader series of attacks perpetrated by groups of gamers against various subjects, including academics studying the medium of the video game. These were accused of promoting an allegedly feminist agenda, and therefore of constituting a threat to the freedom of expression in the production of video games.

At the time of writing, the hashtag GamerGate is still active and largely used on Twitter and other social networks. Although the story surrounding it is becoming lost, it is one of the darkest and most depressing moments in the recent history of video game culture. GamerGate had many novel traits, as well as others that merely repeated similar attacks against women. For instance, it is well known that the video game industry is rife with misogyny, being traditionally male oriented in the marketing of its products and in the composition of the workforce. It has been estimated that 22 percent of workers in the video game industry are women, while consumers are now more or less evenly split (Makuch 2014a, 2014b; Jayanth 2014). GamerGate resembles other misogynist campaigns against inclusivity and representation, seen as false myths of anti-libertarian ideologies. On the other hand, GamerGate also has its unique elements. The use of Twitter, Reddit, YouTube and 4chan simultaneously by a large number of users organised around the same campaign and for such an extended period is unprecedented. Also, it is the first time that an extended anti-feminist movement has occurred in video game culture. Indeed, it was not necessary to experience GamerGate to learn that aggressive behaviours are often targeted against women, and against those who are disempowered, and that academia is often seen as an elitist ivory tower of conspirators.

GamerGate started appearing as a Twitter hashtag when game designer Zoe Quinn was accused of having a conflict of interest with a game journalist for the online gaming magazine *Kotaku* – a publication that is seen by the gaming community as a respectable source of industry news and reviews. The conflict of interest involved her relationship with one of the journalists working at *Kotaku*, an affair that many thought could have biased the reviews of Quinn's games written by the same journalist. It did not matter to the attackers, at the time, that the journalist had never reviewed or commented on any of Quinn's video games on *Kotaku*. The supposed controversy escalated in a series of personal attacks against Quinn, seen as a cheater who had seduced a journalist with the intention of receiving positive reviews for her games. Quinn was in her own turn supported by several scholars and journalists who defended her position, as the attacks were aimed at her as a woman in the game industry rather than for any evident wrongdoing.

In the same period, one defender in particular, Anita Sarkeesian, released a series of YouTube videos exposing the objectification of women in games and in work placements, and took a stand in favour of Quinn. The series, titled Tropes vs. Women, analysed the repetition of the same stereotypical representations of women across a large variety of video games, for instance as damsels in distress to be saved by the male hero, or as rewards for the male character at the end of the quest (feministfrequency 2016). Sarkeesian became another character to be put under the spotlight by the GamerGate campaign, because her series was seen by many as an attempt to influence the representation of women in games and limit the freedom of expression of the (male) video game programmers. GamerGate soon became a campaign against both Quinn and Sarkeesian, and then escalated into a broader campaign against women and feminists, who were seen as threatening the status quo. The threat posed by women, according to the perpetrators of GamerGate, was mostly defined as a limitation to freedom of expression by imposing standards for the representation of women in video games.

As the campaign went on, the series of attacks also included the Digital Games Research Association (DiGRA), an academic organisation that gathers scholars who investigate topics surrounding the medium of the video game. DiGRA was seen as joining in this feminist conspiracy and receiving funds from lobbies and pressure groups in order to justify and promote the inclusion (or intrusion) of women in game culture. Shira Chess and Adrienne Shaw report how minutes taken during a session on GamerGate at the DiGRA 2014 conference were uploaded on an open Google Document and subsequently found and misused by those who supported the conspiracy theories. Many understood the references to identity and diversity contained in the document as evidence of an organised agenda to influence the video game industry, and attacked the two organisers of the session for being involved in such a conspiracy (Chess and Shaw 2015). The two scholars started receiving personal attacks, and saw their document being quoted by gamers to demonstrate the presence of a link between DiGRA, the American government and the major video game publishers. They were also accused of organising 'Communist meetings [in the] halls of academia' (Sargon of Akkad 2014).

Like a Parasite to Gaming

In the last two years, I have been following many online discussions grouped under the GamerGate hashtag. There have been countless threads on Reddit and 4chan, and thousands of tweets sent every hour. The most common theme of these discussions was that of conspiracy, often accompanied by detailed explanations of how women, journalists, politicians and industry experts (often seen as unified actors with particular agendas) were allegedly plotting to destroy the medium of the video game for the sake of gender equality.

While I was lazily scrolling a long thread on Reddit, titled 'People are now claiming that GamerGate is killing gaming archiving' (azsuranil 2015), I found a comment that broke the wall separating myself, on the other side of the screen, and the story being narrated. While I was reading these comments as an external observer, I became part of the story because of a post by a user named koyima, who was directly accusing people like me of shaping the debate surrounding GamerGate while pretending to be outsiders. The comment put academia under the spotlight for having interests in influencing the perception of the general public against the category of gamers. In a purely conspiratorial fashion, most of the respondents to that comment had something to say about how academics are trying to change the game industry and are personally profiting from doing so. It is worth quoting the comment in full:

Academia is like a parasite to gaming at the moment. They produce nothing, they just try to make money and papers (prestige) off other people's work. Usually by trying to shred it through a biased perspective that has no real application IRL [in real life].

koyima (2015)

Being part of academia myself, I felt that I should respond. In fact, and as I will discuss throughout this chapter, I found the comment to be appropriate in its description of what I do, although I disagree with the post's pejorative tone. As I will argue, being a parasite is not a bad position at all, and it can be useful to think of ourselves as parasites when deciding how differently the stories of GamerGate could also be read: by breaking the dualisms and oppositions that have defined the debate so far, and introducing the problem of being always and necessarily in between factions, never fully inside but neither completely detached, like parasites with their host organisms.

In my job I do not produce anything tangible (if not in the form of printed books). The words I write, and the presentations and lectures I give, have no material presence. In that sense, the user koyima is right in saying that 'They produce nothing'. However, such production of nothing would be certainly much more laudable than the production of something, if that something is violent, oppressive, sexist or racist. Moreover, being a producer of nothing puts me in good company. Those who work in finance, for example, are regularly accused of gathering every morning in the financial centres of the world (Wall Street, Canary Wharf, and so on), mostly to produce nothing. Yet, their nothing has dramatic consequences for the lives of many. As with finance, academia has the peculiar ability of producing a kind of nothing which can be extremely influential, persuasive and effective. Also, in both cases, producing nothing must not be misunderstood as the result of a sort of intellectual laziness: usually both academics and brokers are extremely busy and tend to work outside the typical 9 to 5 schedule. What keeps us busy is not the production of tangible outcomes but the continuous reassemblage and reshaping of already existing things (concepts and money, respectively). In the case of academics, our job often involves the retelling of stories, facts and ideas through a different framework. In this sense, koyima is right in saying that we look at 'other people's work', and produce nothing by ourselves. However, we are not the exception, we are not necessarily always looking for 'money' and 'prestige', and we even might occasionally have an impact 'IRL' (in real life).

But we certainly are parasites. This needs to be unpacked, of course, as there are many different kinds of parasites, some of which are necessary or even beneficial to the hosting organism. In biology, parasites are merely seen as living at the expense of other beings, but the definition can be broadened to include forms of symbiotic relation wherein both the parasite and the host affect each other. Michel Serres has identified in the parasite a key figure in understanding the processes of communication exchange, to the point that he has dedicated an entire work to the topic (Serres 1982). Serres argues that the figure of the parasite, as well as the *hôte* (which means, in French, both host and guest), has both a social and a biological function that cannot be reduced to mere passivity. According to Serres, the parasite makes communication possible, being an element of interruption which is both external to the system and part of it. Any system, Serres argues, tends to be corrupted or interrupted by external factors. There is no chance that in the long term it can be kept closed and preserved as it is.

According to Serres, parasites are not only the louse or the rat but anything that is at the same time internal and external to a system. In the words of Lawrence Schehr, translator of *The Parasite*:

The parasite is a microbe, an insidious infection that takes without giving and weakens without killing. The parasite is also a guest, who exchanges his talk, praise, and flattery for food. The parasite is noise as well, the static in a system or the interference in a channel. These seemingly dissimilar activities are, according to Michel Serres, not merely coincidentally expressed by the same word (in French). Rather, they are intrinsically related and, in fact, they have the same basic function in a system. Whether it produces a fever or just hot air, the parasite is a thermal exciter. And as such, it is both the atom of a relation and the production of a change in this relation.

Schehr (1982, x)

Serres explains the role played by the parasite by turning to the image of the *hôte*, at the same time guest and host. A *hôte* receives and consumes, 'gives and receives, offers and accepts, invites and is invited, master and passer-by' (Serres 1982, 15). This relation is always going to be unsettled by noise and interruptions, by the arrival of a further parasite. The parasite is that which introduces complexity and expels the present *hôte*, introducing a new relation and becoming a new *hôte*. According to Serres, the alleged linearity of the communication process is not only inadequate but also subverts the more correct hierarchy in which noise and parasites are the defining factors of communication. Parasites are not just others or external exploiters; they are also those entities that define the system by giving it a new structure.

Lecturers are indeed parasites, as many denigrators of the ivory tower of academia often say, but possibly of the good kind. We are not completely part of what we study, nor are we external to it. Rather we are dependent on and at the same time influencing what we look at, as the *hôte* presented by Serres. I believe that the role and presence of parasites has been largely undervalued, if not ignored, in the accounts surrounding GamerGate. In fact, GamerGate has been mostly narrated as the story of a change in the gaming landscape where a new category of consumers (namely, women, but also other groups that were previously considered to be marginal) is now replacing the old one (the male teenage gamers). As I will argue, this view has a problem with evaluating the presence of parasites. First, it underestimates the necessity of being somehow always in between rather than fully part of an identifiable faction. Moreover, it undervalues the role played by the voices, neither internal nor external to game culture, which actively reframe and give new shape to the system by explaining how this change is allegedly happening. In these stories about new categories of consumers replacing others, there is no account of how these categories co-exist, and who is responsible for deciding who or what they are.

Gamers Are Dead

As GamerGate reached its lowest point in the denigration of women, many commentators argued that this might have been caused by the progressive disappearance of the traditional gamer as a consumer of video games. GamerGate was described as the final violent reaction of gamers before their complete disappearance. Leigh Alexander on Gamasutra (28 August 2014) titled an article 'Gamers Don't Have to Be Your Audience. Gamers Are Over'. In this article, rapidly commented on and linked by many other sources, Alexander argued that a much more varied group of consumers is now emerging, to the point where game developers should stop worrying about addressing their products to the male teenagers that were once responsible for the great majority of sales (2014).

Dan Golding, academic and blogger, wrote a post on the same day about the end of gamers. As Golding puts it: '[gamers] have astutely, and correctly identified what is going on here. Their toys *are* being taken away . . . Videogames now live in the world and there is no going back. I am convinced that this marks the end. We are finished here. From now on, there are no more gamers – only players' (Golding 2014). Golding was writing from the first-person view of a gamer accepting his own end, and welcoming a new scenario where people like him were no longer the majority. His appeal was also directed to those who perpetuated the GamerGate campaign, asking them to stop and move on, accepting their own defeat.

Both articles, influential in the following days on social networks, depicted a sad representation of gamers: a minority that seeks confirmation for its aggressive and oppressive behaviour against an emerging and wider audience of players, which is apparently making gamers disappear to the point where they are no longer relevant. However, claiming that gamers are over can hardly represent an inclusive approach towards those who, for example, currently identify with the hard-core community but equally disagree with the aggressive stance of the so-called 'social justice warriors'. The GamerGate controversy ended up denouncing an aggressive behaviour that might equally be reappropriated by the new audiences (or whoever speaks for them), particularly if it is seen as a winner-takes-all scenario where a new majority is supplanting the previous one. Not coincidentally, I believe, many of the claims about the end of gamers have been supported by market research statistics from various organisations and institutions, all showing that female gamers were officially the majority, or very close to becoming so. Sales figures and pie charts were used to demonstrate and reveal the supposed reality of such a defeat for male gamers, as if it were a fact to be supported by quantitative research. The rhetoric of the death of gamers and the victory of the new challenger prepared a narrative of us-against-them which was equally adopted by the discourses of GamerGate supporters.

Moreover, Microsoft and Sony have attempted to appeal to a wider and more profitable market in recent years by addressing a more solid base of consumers with varied tastes (a similar direction to that taken by Nintendo with its Wii console in 2006). Hard-core gamers have criticised this choice. From this point of view, the conspiracies around GamerGate could receive further support and reinforce the narrative of opposition between the gamers and the establishment, represented by industry experts, scholars and commentators. Finally, and most importantly, the defence of the rights of women to be represented in video games in a respectful way, and to take part in the industry with fair salaries and the same rights as men, cannot be justified by the emergence of a market sector: it should be achieved regardless of the number of women involved, and not because of them supposedly becoming a majority.

GamerGate must be condemned, but not through the same oppositions framed by its supporters. This is firstly because those who feel betrayed by the video game industry would interpret those claims as a confirmation of their paranoid fear of a global feminist–academic–industrial conspiracy. In addition, these arguments replicate the same structure of discourse produced by gamers who now feel marginalised. The problem is not that these might represent false analyses of the reality of video game culture; the problem stems from the aggressive (and masculine) gesture that underlies the very idea that video game culture could be truthfully analysed. Defenders of GamerGate have set an aggressive tone by claiming to know the truth about what video games really are, and to whom they belong. But the same approach could be replicated by those who critique the movement. After all, how are these stories about the presence of women in games appearing to us? How does the truth about the alleged changes in the gaming landscape come to be constructed as such?

Roberta Williams, a Woman in Game History

Laine Nooney poses similar questions in a paper on the reception of the story and personal life of game designer Roberta Williams, and re-enables a more destabilising, anxious account of the emergence and presence of women in the game industry (Nooney 2013). Nooney looks at the historiographies of the medium and questions the 'practice of "adding women on" ' (1) to the history of video games: reconstructions of the key figures of the industry tend to shape the image of a male-dominated context in which women appear only occasionally, as extra characters. The narratives around Roberta Williams are viewed by Nooney as an excellent example of this apparent opening towards women in games. Roberta Williams was the co-founder, with her husband Ken Williams, of Sierra On-Line, and was one of the most celebrated game designers of the 1980s and 1990s. However, she was neither a programmer nor a gamer. In an interview with Williams, reported by Nooney, the game designer confesses: 'I don't program, and I'm not technical, and I'm not even a game player. So you know, everybody says, "Well what are you doing in this industry?" [*Laughter*]' (14).

Acknowledging that 'history is not in what we talk about, but in *how we organize its meaning*' (Nooney 2013, 3), Nooney asks the following questions: '*why* is Roberta Williams [in game history] in the ways that she is? What can Roberta Williams tell us *about* game history? How is it that she became an object *of* game history?' (4). Nooney focuses on how historiographies of video games have been written. Her questions regard the modalities for talking about the history of games and gamers. Williams is presented as a non-gamer in the historical reconstructions, a strange character who is influential and well known and yet difficult to categorise. Williams defines herself as a strange case, recognising the impossibility of fitting herself into the typical figure of the male, computer-savvy game designer. However, her discomfort (a feeling Nooney describes through documents of different kinds, including photos with other famous game designers in which Williams clearly feigns excitement and appears out of context) does not simply derive from being a female character in a male-dominated context. In fact, Williams had been included as a female game designer even in the contemporary accounts of the game industry. Williams fits into game histories only as an extra, a token for women and games. Yet Williams apparently did not know how to use a computer, had no experience of software tools and worked by herself, from home, while taking care of her children. Nooney imagines the kitchen table to be the space where Williams designed, with pen and paper, most of the games to be converted into digital format later by her assistants. The space of the kitchen is seen by Nooney not just as a collection of furniture, objects and allowances. The kitchen is not simply a different workstation. It is a gendered space in which Williams used to work in a manner that could not be understood by the histories of the video game industry. The presumption of these historical reconstructions was that game designers must be gamers, that is, perfectly capable of using computers and even pushing the limits of those technologies. However, those discourses shaped the figure of the gamer as a subject to which Williams could not conform. As Nooney puts it:

When we inquire into 'what counts' in game history, that question is beyond the immediately apparent: it is also about how history arrives. How do spaces, bodies and objects entangle to produce a historical subject – and why do we presume that this subject is a 'gamer'?

Nooney (2013, 10)

If GamerGate is an event in the history of the medium, then it appears to be an event that changes the role of women in video game culture, by giving them legitimacy to speak, as if women were *happening* in the medium of the video game. But then the question is: who is making them happen? How are women entering the history of the medium? Or to refashion the same methodological question posed by Nooney, 'why are women in the history of gaming in the way they are?'

Nooney hints that such emergence of women in games is not just due to a change in market audience of the game industry, as Alexander and Golding argued later in regard to GamerGate. It also concerns issues of power and legitimacy to speak. Stories about the medium of the video game are *not all equally present.*

The comment left on Reddit which suggested that we academics are all parasites should now be taken seriously and pushed to its full extent. We can exercise our role as parasites in gaming by looking at the spaces in between, the co-existence of various voices that exploit each other and live in symbiotic interdependence. There are stories about the medium, and about the role of women in games. Some of these are granted a position of legitimacy, and others are not. However, these co-exist, albeit differently, and if I want to be a good *hôte* I need to find ways of becoming hospitable, and a good guest. How can I become a parasite of the good kind, and question the processes of mutual interaction that make collectivities, identities and conflicts come into being?

The voices reported so far, which have discussed and analysed the presence of women in games, act as parasites in their own turn: they transform without producing, they exploit by living at the boundaries of the systems they observe. Yet, these actors of transformation, which in previous chapters I have referred to by other names (hackers, mediators and hybrids), are also there as ethical subjects: the *hôte* can be good and bad, they can be welcoming and exclusionary, beneficial or lethal to the organism. Voices about the medium of the video game and its participants can easily adopt the tone of the patriarchal narrators critiqued by Nooney and accept divergences from their allegedly transparent and linear stories of the medium, but only as long as these are exceptions, as happened in the case of Roberta Williams. However, to take up the suggestion from the commentator on Reddit, we need to find our own way of becoming a different kind of parasite, a good *hôte.*

Conclusion: Women in Games, Women and Games

In recent years there have been a number of initiatives in relation to the inclusion of women in the production of video games. In the United Kingdom, the Women in Games initiative organises game jam sessions where women can gather, learn how to make a game and have a final product by the end of the session, which usually lasts for one or two days. Only women are allowed to take part in order to provide them with a welcoming space for learning, without the pressure of the supposed hierarchies of skill and competency conventionally attributed to gender. The Women in Games initiative also responds to similar programmes that have occurred elsewhere but could not eliminate the social barriers that emerge whenever skills are thought to be differently distributed. Stephanie Fisher and Alison Harvey have noticed how the Difference Engine Initiative (DEI), taking place in Toronto, Canada, had similarly good intentions regarding the inclusion of women in the production of independent video games but failed in its purpose (Fisher and Harvey 2013). Toronto has become, in recent years, one of the most prolific cities in terms of game production, but the industry is still largely dominated by male programmers. Consequently, initiatives oriented to women have been welcomed as inclusive and progressive. However, Fisher and Harvey argue that leaving the organisation of the event in the hands of those same male figures who currently dominate in the industry effectively put the guests in a difficult position: the learning activity was no longer taking place between peers but instead was being directed by a higher authority towards a certain number of guests.

Fisher and Harvey's analysis is relevant to the GamerGate case, because it sheds light on how inclusivity and representation become political issues:

Undertaking interventionist work to break down barriers is imperative to opening up a culture to the disenfranchised, but can also be potentially problematic when the existing and largely *invisible* power relations and structures that organize these relations are not explicitly recognized in the planning, implementation, or analysis of these interventions. Even the best-intentioned programs, practices, and people operate within the racist, heterosexist, patriarchal, and capitalist hegemonic orders they seek to topple.

(2013, 29)

As the authors suggest, DEI was organised in a way that made it almost impossible to tell different stories about the meanings and values of game design. Telling different stories, and letting others tell their own story, is precisely the alternative practice that can destabilise the existing relations of power, while offering a context in which to be good parasites. I propose, in this respect, that we think about the presence of women less as a process of inclusion of diversities, and more radically as a rewriting of the histories of gaming.

There is a difference between thinking about women *in* games and about women *and* games. Thinking in terms of women *in* games still assumes an abstract unified character of women, which is now allegedly stepping into the history of gaming, thus assuming also a source of power that grants legitimacy to entering such a history. After all, letting someone *in* is a patriarchal gesture, as it assumes the presence of a gatekeeper who decides who or what can come in.[1] Roberta Williams's story is an example of the same problem, as she was allowed to enter but only as a token for those excluded and left outside by the dominant politics of video game historiographies.

Telling different stories is also a way of re-evaluating the parasites. Parasites are neither in nor out, but in between and next to. Parasites are not gatekeepers, but might live at the door, or at the window: at the margins and boundaries. Organisms *live with* parasites, and are parasites in their own turn. As I discussed in previous chapters in relation to my engagement with NikeFuel, and when looking at the stories of the independent developers and the hackers of PlayStation Network, once again I believe that the problem lies in the ethical question of finding good and better ways of living together for gamers and games.

Thus, thinking in terms of women *and* games, instead, means looking at the many different characters that are currently approaching games as players, designers, commentators and scholars (often, in fact, mixing and confusing these different roles). Women *and* video games can do very different things; they can contribute in a variety of ways that do not necessarily conform to the expected behaviours and interests of the official history of the medium. Roberta Williams, as much as Zoe Quinn and Anita Sarkeesian, cannot make much sense as women *in* the official history of the medium except by confirming its patriarchal ideology that sees men as

---

[1] The observation does not mean to be a critique of the Women in Games initiative, which is instead very aware of the power relations at stake in issues of inclusivity. However, I suggest that the initiative could be more appropriately named with a conjunction rather than a preposition.

preceding and authorising the arrival of other characters. However, they make sense as women who approach digital games with their own perspectives and interests. While *being with* video games, they are effectively rewriting the history (and future) of gaming.

There are many examples of women *and* games. I am thinking of the work of Anna Anthropy, who is a game designer, author and commentator of contemporary events of game culture. Anthropy also tries to present personal and intimate stories through her games, mostly made using open-source production tools such as Twine, and released for free on her own website. In one of her most famous games, *Dys4ia*, she provocatively presents a playable account of her own life experience when she decided to pursue hormone replacement therapy. This is only one of the many examples where Anthropy uses game design to tell personal stories, stories that have no resolution, no moral, but that certainly share a sense of being in trouble.

What is most relevant in the production of Anna Anthropy is that she is not asking to be part of the official histories of gaming. In fact, she is writing her own history. Quite literally, as she has also started her own archive to preserve digitally video games that she believes to be interesting for herself and worth saving – of course, many of these games are rarely on the radar of the most widespread knowledge of gaming history. On Anna Archive, she collects various sorts of video games: from abandoned software to pre-Internet online gaming, and scanned copies of magazines, booklets, posters and role-playing books. Each element of the archive offers a glimpse of an alternative perspective on the history of game culture, one that defies the tales of technological progress and the fossilised representations of gender.

Anna Anthropy is not a woman *in* game culture, she is a woman rewriting her own personal history of the medium by doing, thinking, talking about games, and making them too. Anthropy's history of gaming is a history with no fathers, no mothers and no parents. She asks herself and takes responsibility for what to make and which games to preserve. Her history has no teleology; it has unknown solutions and takes multiple personal directions, as it involves her as curator in the process of its own writing.

If there is one thing that we (gamers, players, scholars, authors and so on) could learn from GamerGate, it is that we need to take responsibility for what we necessarily are: parasites in gaming. And since we are, and have always been, implicated in this game as exploiters and exploited, we should find the most hospitable way to play our role. Chess and Shaw reach relevant conclusions in their account of how their research on GamerGate was misinterpreted by GamerGaters, generating a further wave of hate and conspiracy theories (Chess and Shaw 2015). They argue that the misunderstanding was caused by a blog post by Andrew Grant Wilson, which stated 'we talked a big game at DiGRA about dismantling hegemonic masculinity' (Wilson 2014). The sentence was taken as evidence of a plan to influence video game culture from the ivory tower of academia. However, conspiracy theories are usually spread by, and say something about, those who feel disempowered, as Chess and Shaw argue. The authors try to find what connects the aggressors with the medium they both study and are passionate about, and identify a common ground from where to understand and dismantle, as part of the same gesture, hegemonic masculinity. Once again, the ethical question emerges from acknowledging our marginal position, asking ourselves not just who we are, but how we are related to others.

In August 2016, I gave a talk at the DiGRA conference at Abertay University, in Dundee, Scotland, on the same topic as this chapter. In April 2017, the abstract of my talk was published on Reddit and dissected by its users in a thread in the section dedicated to 'social justice'.[2] The comments are unanimously disparaging of my intervention, and one of them makes the point that the academic parasite is not welcome, as they 'don't want to give [their] biological organisms new shapes'. I argue that preserving the shape of video game culture is also an attempt at controlling its future. It is another way of claiming the authority to decide what game culture is and what it becomes. However, in the present, there are countless parasites that sit at the margins of this culture, including the other dozens of authors who contribute to the same thread. They are all writing, as I am, meaning that dividing them into collective subjects such as 'we' and 'them' is becoming increasingly difficult: any voice that makes claims about video game culture is necessarily parasitical and performing the role of the authority that decides for the others. For this reason it is important not to be oppressive

---

[2] The thread is available at https://redd.it/63sx86 (last accessed 7 May 2017).

when formulating statements on the supposed reality of game culture, and possibly leave the door open at all times.

To become parasites in gaming means rewriting its history, telling different stories and making *different differences* between the stories we already know. In the end, we might 'produce nothing', but we might become better hosts and guests for whoever comes next.

Conclusion: At the Time of Writing

Writing the conclusion to a book brings with it a certain amount of anxiety. While looking back at what I have done so far, I cannot help but think about what lies ahead. From the time I submit this manuscript, the process of reviewing, editing and publication will take at least one year. By that time, the examples and references that I have discussed in this book will be one year older, if not more, and might have been surpassed by more recent examples and events that make my argument look obsolete. Writing takes time, and publishing takes even longer.

On the other hand, there is a fast mutating gaming industry, which produces and consumes products at high speed. A video game can be considered old just a few months after its release. Games are replaced by sequels almost on a yearly basis, or they get updated every few weeks. This is particularly evident in the market of smartphone games, which are typically modified by their original producers through frequent software updates. Production tools such as Twine make it possible to design a game and release it in a few hours. Video game culture is composed of texts produced at different speeds, and writing about gamers and games has its own temporality and duration. In such a rapidly changing scenario, it seems that every game, console, article and academic text is always catching up, necessarily out of date before its release or publication.

At the time of writing this conclusion, a new game has been released which seems to confuse once again the definition of a video game, potentially forcing me to reconsider some of the arguments in my work. *Pokémon Go*, developed by Niantic, is presented by many sources as a new successful mobile app, already downloaded millions of times across the globe, and which is expected to set new standards for the genre of alternative reality games. *Pokémon Go* develops the popular Pokémon series, originally developed by Nintendo. Niantic was previously affiliated with Google, and worked with them at the game *Ingress*, which largely inspired the production of *Pokémon Go*. *Pokémon Go* builds on the game *Ingress* in its concept and design, and reuses some of the graphical elements of the previous game. Both games are based on the same idea: players are supposed to play the game on their (Internet-connected and GPS-enabled) smartphones to move around the streets of their city in the real world, checking specific spots to collect elements of the game and to challenge other players in designated areas. *Pokémon Go* represents a more recent example of the (thus far unsuccessful) genre of alternative reality games, where the ludic environment blurs with the urban context in which the players live. *Pokémon Go* re-adapts the pre-existing large number of fictional monsters (the Pokémon, short for pocket monsters, which players try to capture, train, evolve and bring to battle with the Pokémon of other players). The use of an already famous brand, which immediately attracted fans of the series from all over the world, has proven to be a particularly successful decision for Niantic. Thus, the immediate popularity of *Pokémon Go* is to be attributed to the combination of an old brand with original design elements.

The rapid success of the game has prompted many to comment on the reasons behind its popularity, its possible future developments and the implications of the rise of alternative reality games. The first reactions seemed to betray a concern about the risks associated with walking around while keeping one's eyes on a screen. Initial articles published after the release of the game reported stories of players falling into pits, risking their lives walking near cliffs to catch a rare Pokémon, or getting robbed while adventuring alone at night (Serhan 2016; Bastow 2016; Romano 2016). Omari Akil commented on *Medium* magazine about the risks for black people playing *Pokémon Go* in the United States, where police are easily called whenever a person of colour is seen walking around in circles in the same area (Akil 2016). Others commented on the supposed health benefits of playing *Pokémon Go* (Armanet 2016). The game encourages video game players – stereotypically thought of as people with sedentary lifestyles – to walk outside for long distances, in what could possibly become a game that makes them lose weight and increase their levels of vitamin

D by exposing them to sunlight (Ryder 2016). Last but not least, there was an immediate warning (by the film director Oliver Stone, no less) that the game collects private data about the user, with the potential to sell it on to private companies (Press Association 2016). Shops and cafes, in turn, are offered the opportunity to pay Niantic to have a rare Pokémon in their stores, thus attracting the desired kind of players/consumers towards their businesses.

These somewhat banal stories about the novelty of *Pokémon Go* offer scenarios in which the newness of the game is presented through narratives that are fairly familiar to anyone already interested in digital gaming, and digital media in general. Questions around the benefits or damage of video games to one's health have been around since the medium first became popular. Atari products were seen, in the late 1970s, to cause damage to the skin, muscles and brains of their players, and were feared as giving rise to an entire generation of teenagers with physical deformations caused by prolonged gaming sessions.[1] Conversely, the gamification trend has promoted the idea that video games might be beneficial for their players, as the act of playing forces them to move – both physically and intellectually. Moreover, it is now commonly acknowledged that digital technologies invade users' privacy, collect and resell personal data, and ultimately that video games are business products, made to be either commercially released or to make profits from the users' behaviour as they play.[2]

There is a strange dissonance between the timing of my own writing and that of the narratives around new video game products. The rapid succession of releases and updates, and the many voices that define what

---

[1] Narratives around the effects of video games on health have been explored by the Game Arthritis series, by artists Matteo Bittanti and IOCOSE (2011). In the series, the medical studies on the imagined effects of video games have been represented in a fictional and uncanny photographic documentation. Ultimately, the series provokes questions about the conditions for saying the truth about the effects of video games on our bodies and minds. The project is available at http://gamearthritis.org (last accessed 30 January 2017).

[2] As I write, a digital company is already combining all these stories about health and privacy into a new business opportunity. *PokeFit* is a new app which connects the data collected by *Pokémon Go* and visualises information for the user who wants to get fitter and healthier. Indeed, the same data is then resold to other companies for marketing purposes (Chang 2016).

these changes are and what they mean, seem to imply their own failure while presenting themselves as new. These stories suggest that whatever is presented as new is not new at all, and that the same economic, cultural and social conditions for making and playing games are preserved in the apparently new scenario (Orland 2016). The future of gaming is narrated as being so similar to the present as to make it already *boring*: already experienced, always so-last-year.

It is significant that as soon as *Pokémon Go* had been released, articles proliferated in the gaming community about what might be included in the first update of the game. Some argued that the possibility of exchanging Pokémon between users might become a feature, or that player rankings divided by geographical region might be introduced (Pope 2016; Frank 2016). As noted by Wendy Chun, the update is the necessary result of the accelerating cycles of use and production of digital products, which imply that users' habits must face their own periodic crises. Thus, everything must always 'update to stay the same', to be immediately rewritten and transformed into another cycle of 'habit + crisis' (Chun 2016). *Pokémon Go* is no exception, and the imagined crisis of the game was narrated (one might say, following Grusin 2010, 'premediated') as soon as the game was released, expecting it to disappoint even before it could exist. Or, more radically and tragically, the failure of *Pokémon Go* has been necessary for its own existence.

At the time of writing, there seems already to be nothing left to say or imagine about a video game released only a few days ago. How can writing cope with these rapid and repetitive cycles of excitement and boredom, so common if not intrinsic to video game and digital culture? The tales of technological innovation appear to be out of time: they repeat the same questions and answers, offering us very similar narratives that become quickly predictable, to the point that it takes only one or two days to exhaust any possibility of what *Pokémon Go* could signify – or any other product which irrupts into the market and is welcomed as having elements of originality. These stories present the medium of the video game as orbiting in a vacuum, a space where nothing matters and everything has already been seen.

In the project outlined in the Introduction, I offered an approach to the study of video games which I named Creative Game Studies. Ultimately,

I believe that Creative Game Studies can be a method for thinking of interventions within game culture as organised around the timing of writing. Creative Game Studies is made of interventions that use to their own advantage the dissonant pace and rhythm that differentiates the practice of writing from the cadence of the stories of progression and crisis of the medium of the video game. Indeed, these cyclical stories of the medium are written, too. But the timing of their writing is made to disappear by presenting these stories as if they belonged to nowhere and had no relation to the time of their production and reception.

In the Introduction, I presented Creative Game Studies as *intuitive, timely, performative, ethical, anti-authoritarian* and *anxious*. Ultimately, the notion of *being creative* captures them all. Being creative appears to be an imperative nowadays for anyone who lives within a neoliberal economy (and some may argue that 'anyone' really means 'everyone', as there seems to be no outside to neoliberalism). In Creative Game Studies, creativity implies involvement and participation. Both aspects are made to disappear in the context of neoliberal economies, in which the sense of being creative mostly means becoming a productive individual capable of adapting at the expense of others (thus, it mostly means being alone). Creativity as participation and involvement leads to a mode of writing which pays attention to the where-and-when of the act of enunciation. It also means being ethically responsible for those people and things we write about, and with. It inscribes writing in the environment, thus making it performative and constitutive of the reality surrounding the text. It questions the dualisms and categories of the common-sense discourses around technologies and the sources of power that grant them legitimacy and authority. Finally, it means being anxiously at stake in the process of writing.

I have evoked the notion of creativity throughout this book, when looking at the narratives of engagement (Chapter 1) and independence (Chapter 2), when exploring the notion of network and hacking (Chapter 3), archaeology (Chapter 4) and of the parasite (Chapter 5). These notions have been developed to problematise my own presence in the text, to speak in terms of relationships rather than objects, and responsibilities rather than agencies. Through Creative Game Studies we can once again play *with* video games: in their company, while making them and transforming ourselves.

In the first chapter, I imagined an alternative narrative of engagement with gamification, by looking at how relationships with gamified technologies mutate in time. In the future, it is unlikely that we will be using video games to improve our health, or to fix the problems of the world, but we might have to live with digital forms of quantification of the self, and this might not even be presented to us as a deliberate choice. In fact, the problem of engaging with games already affects our contemporary lives, and writing alternative narratives of engagement could be a survival strategy for the present. The understanding of time and movement implicated in practices of gamification appears to eliminate any form of change and becoming. In my intervention, I imagine more lively engagement with gamification, understanding it in terms of kinship, and re-evaluating its mutations and accidents.

The notion of independence similarly implies movement and change in the life of the developers who decide to find alternative routes to make and release a video game. However, it appears to create an unsolvable condition of undecidability for those who profess to be part of it. Yet, the impossibility of defining independence is a productive force, which brings developers to discourses of self-definition and, potentially, openness towards others. It is unlikely that new tools of video game production and distribution will bring many aspiring authors to be successful and autonomous in the near future. My intervention has consisted in looking at the contemporary discourses of independence, questioning their structures, and introducing the problem of the other: that which is implied in the act of claiming one's own independence, and which could be represented by the video game industry, the other independents, or one's own game. I have proposed that in these discursive performances, the notion of independence is constructed and continuously undoes itself. It is in the present that the ethical problem of taking care of others emerges in the narratives of independent game development.

The notion of the present and future of the medium is also explored in the third chapter, where I looked at the story of the hacking of PlayStation Network as another case in which the definition of games is contested. The definition of what PlayStation 3 is, who has control over it, and what its physical boundaries are, became a framework within which one could make decisions over one's own freedom in relation to a video game console. The defence by Sony's attorney in the trial against the corporation resulted in a definition of video game products that foregrounds time and power as key factors, involving the speaker and her time in the boundaries of a video game console. However, these processes of involvement and manipulation happen all the time, as hackers manipulate consoles and players play with them. Consoles and networks leak, but it matters how we decide to join in the hacking of these assemblages of words and silicon, and what kind of freedom we intend to claim for ourselves.

The future of video games is also written by reconstructing its history, and deciding which questions matter the most when looking at the origins of the medium. In the fourth chapter I looked at how the archaeological excavations of *E.T.*, while trying to freeze the past and future of gaming through the structures of the present, instead revealed the impossibility of saying the truth about the history of the medium. I have turned to Foucault's concept of genealogy to uncover the instability of the present, and to show how writing about the history of video games becomes part of it. However, it matters how we relate to the present. Foucault's notion of genealogy was intended to challenge the categories and groupings of contemporary discursive formations rather than reinforce them. Not all excavations are the same, as they can reveal different histories, and frame different futures.

In the fifth chapter I considered another event within game culture where the past, present and future of gaming was challenged, by questioning the authorities that write about what it is and what it can become. The GamerGate controversy generated forms of harassment against women in game culture. Academia was also accused of attempting to take control of a culture that could allegedly belong only to a limited category of consumers. However, writing what video game culture is, was and could be is always and necessarily a parasitical practice: it exploits and gives, it modifies the context it writes about while being at the same time involved in it, by living at its margins. Thus, writing and making video games should not be seen as a way of entering or stepping into game culture, or as a gesture that requires permission from, or is granted access by, others. Instead, it is a mode of relating to this cultural context, and writing about games, as much as making or playing them, is transformative of video game culture and of the subjects involved. There are examples of women who, precisely because of the difficulty of entering the official accounts of gaming, have already started to write their own parasitical stories, creating alternative futures, possibly more hospitable than the one that sparked the GamerGate campaign.

At stake in all these stories are different modes of writing. Re-evaluating the act of writing is not just a way of praising my own academic position, as writer rather than developer, programmer, or gamer. At the time of writing, more and more students are opting to take academic courses on game design and development. Creative Game Studies is also a method of reminding them that the false opposition between producing and studying, doing and thinking, is harmful and stupid, as it underestimates thoughts and words in their performative potential, and ultimately frustrates and denies the process of self-transformation that is involved in the act of making a game.

In *Pokémon Go*, while the game is loading, there is a warning which asks players to, essentially, not kill themselves while playing: 'Remember to be alert at all times. Stay aware of your surroundings.' With a gentle paraphrasing, in this book I have attempted to be alert *to* all times: the different times and timings of the narratives of the industry, of the act of playing, and the time of thinking and writing about video game culture. In order to do this, it is crucial to be alert to one's surroundings, and to be present in the environment rather than looking at it from a distance. Being creative means being involved, and to be aware that we are and have always been 'implicated in the game . . . caught by the game . . . from the very beginning at stake in the game' (Derrida 1980, 248).

References

Akil, Omari. 2016. Warning: Pokémon Go Is a Death Sentence If You Are a Black Man. *Medium*, 7 July. Accessed 30 January 2017. https://medium.com/mobile-lifestyle/warning-pokemon-go-is-a-death-sentence-if-you-are-a-black-man-acacb4bdae7f#.ffx549ysm.

Alexander, Leigh. 2014. Gamers Don't Have to Be Your Audience: Gamers Are Over. *Gamasutra.com*, 28 August. Accessed 30 January 2017. www.gamasutra.com/view/news/224400/Gamers_dont_have_to_be_your_audience_Gamers_are_over.php.

Anderson, John. 1983. Who Really Invented the Video Game? There Was Bell, There Was Edison, There Was Fermi. And Then There Was Higinbotham. *Creative Computing Video and Arcade Games* Spring issue: 8–11. Accessed 30 January 2017. www.digitpress.com/library/magazines/ccvag/ccvag_spring83.pdf.

Andersson, Jonas. 2009. For the Good of the Net: The Pirate Bay as a Strategic Sovereign. *Culture Machine* 10: 64–108. Accessed 30 January 2017. www.culturemachine.net/index.php/cm/article/view/346/359.

Anthropy, Anna. 2012. *Rise of the Videogame Zinesters: How Freaks, Normals, Amateurs, Artists, Dreamers, Drop-outs, Queers, Housewives, and People Like You Are Taking Back an Art Form*. New York: Seven Stories Press.

Apperley, Thomas, and Jussi Parikka. 2015. Platform Studies' Epistemic Threshold. *Games and Culture*, 13 December: 1–21. doi:10.1177/1555412015616509.

Arendt, Hannah. 1958. *The Human Condition*. Chicago, IL: University of Chicago Press.

Armanet, Jorge. 2016. Could Pokémon Go Improve People's Health? *The Guardian*, 27 July. Accessed 30 January 2017. www.theguardian.com/healthcare-network/2016/jul/27/pokemon-go-improve-health-walking.

Attack of the Show. 2011. Hacking and Jailbreaking with George Hotz. *YouTube*, 14 January. Accessed 30 January 2017. www.youtube.com/watch?v=tG9r7cCpk_g&feature=player_embedded.

Austin, John L. 1962. *How to Do Things with Words*. Oxford: Clarendon Press.

azsuranil. 2015. People Are now Claiming that GamerGate Is Killing Gaming Archiving. *Reddit*, 9 March. Accessed 30 January 2017. www.reddit.com/r/KotakuInAction/comments/2ygk0q/people_are_now_claiming_that_gamergate_is_killing/.

Baker, Liana B., and Jim Finkle. 2011. Sony PlayStation Suffers Massive Data Breach, *Reuters*, 27 April, Accessed 30 January 2017. www.reuters.com/article/2011/04/26/us-sony-stoldendata-idUSTRE73P6WB20110426.

Barbrook, Richard, and Andy Cameron. 1995. The Californian Ideology. *The Hypermedia Research Centre*. Accessed 30 January 2017. www.hrc.wmin.ac.uk/hrc/theory/californianideo/index/t.4.html.

Bastow, Clem. 2016. 'There Is a Rattata in my Bathroom': How Pokémon Go Can Take Over Your Life. *The Guardian*, 9 July. Accessed 30 January 2017. www.theguardian.com/technology/2016/jul/09/pokemon-go-take-over-your-life-game-augmented-reality-nintendo-niantic-labs.

BBC. 2016. This Woman Thinks Playing Video Games Can Heal the World. *BBC*. Accessed 30 January 2017. www.bbc.co.uk/bbcthree/item/244517ff-2861-4486-81f5-3c27e487ff8e.

Bergson, Henri. 2001. *Time and Free Will: An Essay on the Immediate Data of Consciousness*. Mineola, NY: Dover Publications. Originally published in 1913, London: George Allen and Company Ltd.

Bergson, Henri. 2007. *Creative Evolution*. London: Palgrave Macmillan. Originally published in 1911, London: Macmillan.

Bogost, Ian. 2011a. Persuasive Games: Exploitationware. *Gamasutra: The Art and Business of Making Games*, 3 May. Accessed 30 January 2017. www.gamasutra.com/view/feature/134735/persuasive_games_exploitationware.php.

Bogost, Ian. 2011b. *How to Do Things with Videogames*. Minneapolis, MN: University of Minnesota Press.

Bogost, Ian. 2015. Why Gamification Is Bullshit. In *The Gameful World: Approaches, Issues, Applications*, edited by Steffen P. Walz and Sebastian Deterding, 65–80. Cambridge, MA: The MIT Press.

Bolter, David J., and Richard Grusin. 1999. *Remediation: Understanding New Media*. Cambridge, MA: The MIT Press.

Carbone, Marco B., and Paolo Ruffino. 2012. Apocalypse Postponed. Discourses on Video Games from Noxious Objects to Redemptive Devices. *GAME Journal* 1 (1). Accessed 30 January 2017. www.gamejournal.it/apocalypse-postponed-discourses-on-video-games-from-noxious-objects-to-redemptive-devices/.

Carbone, Marco B., and Paolo Ruffino. 2014. Video Game Subcultures: Playing at the Periphery of Mainstream Culture. *GAME Journal* 1 (3). Accessed 26 March 2017. www.gamejournal.it/wp-content/uploads/2014/04/GAME_3_Subcultures_Journal_and_CriticalNotes.pdf.

Carnns, Ann. 2011. The PlayStation Breach: Why You Should Remain Calm. *The New York Times*, 27 April. Accessed 30 January 2017. http://bucks.blogs.nytimes.com/2011/04/27/the-playstation-breach-why-you-should-remain-calm/.

Chang, Lulu. 2016. PokeFit Puts a Healthy Spin on Your 'Pokémon Go' Addiction. *Digital Trends*, 30 July. Accessed 30 January 2017. www.digitaltrends.com/mobile/pokemon-go-pokefit/.

Chess, Shira, and Adrienne Shaw. 2015. A Conspiracy of Fishes, or, How We Learned to Stop Worrying About #GamerGate and Embrace Hegemonic Masculinity. *Journal of Broadcasting and Electronic Media* 59 (1): 208–20. doi:10.1080/08838151.2014.999917.

Chun, Wendy H. K. 2016. *Updating to Remain the Same: Habitual New Media.* Cambridge, MA: The MIT Press.

Crogan, Patrick. 2011. *Gameplay Mode: War, Simulation and Technoculture.* Minneapolis, MN: University of Minnesota Press.

Deleuze, Gilles. 1988. *Bergsonism.* New York: Zone Books. Originally published in 1966, Paris: Presses Universitaires de France.

De Loura, Mark, and Randy Paris. 2013. Don't Just Play on Your Phone: Program It. *The White House*, 9 December. Accessed 30 January 2017. www.whitehouse.gov/blog/2013/12/09/don-t-just-play-your-phone-program-it.

Derrida, Jacques. 1976. *Of Grammatology.* Baltimore, MD: The Johns Hopkins University Press.

Derrida, Jacques. 1980. Structure, Sign, and Play in the Discourse of the Human Sciences. In *Writing and Difference*, 278–94. London: Routledge.

Deterding, Sebastian, Dan Dixon, Rilla Khaled, and Lennart Nacke. 2011. From Game Design Elements to Gamefulness: Defining Gamification. *Proceedings of the 15th International Academic MindTrek Conference*, 9–15. Accessed 30 January 2017. doi:10.1145/2181037.2181040.

Edge. 2011. Sony's Harsh Lessons. *Future Publishing*. Issue 229, July.

Electronic Frontier Foundation. 2016. DRM. *Electronic Frontier Foundation. Defending Your Rights in the Digital World.* Accessed 30 January 2017. www.eff.org/issues/drm.

Ensmenger, Nathan L. 2010. *The Computer Boys Take Over: Computers, Programmers, and the Politics of Technical Expertise.* Cambridge, MA: The MIT Press.

Entertainment Software Association. 2015. E3 2015 Teaser: Experience the Evolution. *YouTube*, 7 June. Accessed 30 January 2017. www.youtube.com/watch?v=GDKG_yoJYao.

European Commission Research and Innovation. 2016. Gaming and Gamification, 14 October. Accessed 30 January 2017. http://ec.europa.eu/research/participants/portal/desktop/en/opportunities/h2020/topics/ict-24-2016.html.

feministfrequency. 2016. Tropes vs Women in Video Games – Season 1. *YouTube*. Accessed 30 January 2017. www.youtube.com/playlist?list=PLn4ob_5_ttEaA_vc8F3fjzE62esf9yP61.

Fisher, Stephanie J., and Alison Harvey. 2013. Intervention for Inclusivity: Gender Politics and Indie Game Development. *Loading. . .* 7 (11): 25–40. Accessed 30 January 2017. http://journals.sfu.ca/loading/index.php/loading/article/viewArticle/118.

Fleming, Jeffrey. 2007. Down the Hyper-Spatial Tube: *Spacewar* and the Birth of Digital Game Culture. In *Gamasutra. The Art and Business of Making Games.* 1 June. Accessed 30 January 2017. www.gamasutra.com/view/feature/129861/down_the_hyperspatial_tube_.php.

Foddy, Bennett. 2014. Indiecade East 2014: State of the Union – Bennett Foddy (Keynote). *YouTube*, 25 February. Accessed 26 March 2017. www.youtube.com/watch?v=7XfCT3jhEC0.

Foucault, Michel. 1970. *The Order of Things: An Archaeology of the Human Sciences.* New York: Pantheon Books.

Foucault, Michel. 1972. *The Archaeology of Knowledge.* New York: Harper & Row.

Foucault, Michel. 1977. *Discipline and Punish: The Birth of the Prison.* London: Penguin Books.

Foucault, Michel. 1978. *The History of Sexuality.* London: Penguin Books.

Foucault, Michel. 1980. *Power/Knowledge: Selected Interviews and Other Writings 1972–1977.* New York: Pantheon Books.

Foucault, Michel. 1991. Nietzsche, Genealogy, History. In *The Foucault Reader*, 76–100. London: Penguin Books. Originally published in 1977, Ithaca, NY: Cornell University Press.

Foucault, Michel. 1998. *Technologies of the Self: A Seminar with Michel Foucault.* Edited by Luther H. Martin, Huck Gutman and Patrick H. Hutton. Amherst, MA: The University of Massachusetts Press.

Foucault, Michel. 2005. *The Hermeneutics of the Subject: Lectures at the College de France 1981–1982.* New York: Palgrave Macmillan.

Frank, Allegra. 2016. Pokémon Go Will Get Trading, Other Features in Updates. *Polygon*, 12 July. Accessed 30 January 2017. www.polygon.com/2016/7/12/12158480/pokemon-go-trading-update.

Fuchs, Mathias. 2014. Predigital Precursors of Gamification. In *Rethinking Gamification*, edited by Mathias Fuchs, Sonia Fizek, Paolo Ruffino and Niklas Schrape. Lueneburg: Meson Press.

Fuchs, Mathias, Sonia Fizek, Paolo Ruffino, and Niklas Schrape. 2014. Introduction. In *Rethinking Gamification*, edited by Mathias Fuchs, Sonia Fizek, Paolo Ruffino and Niklas Schrape, 7–20. Lueneburg: Meson Press.

Galloway, Alexander. 2006. *Gaming: Essays on Algorithmic Culture.* Minneapolis, MN: University of Minnesota Press.

Gaydos, Matt. 2012. Using Video Games to Solve Problems. *The White House*, 15 April. Accessed 30 January 2017. www.whitehouse.gov/blog/2012/04/15/using-video-games-solve-problems.

Geohot. 2011 The Light It Up Contest – Geohot. *YouTube*, 12 February. Accessed 30 January 2017. www.youtube.com/watch?v=9iUvuaChDEg.

Gilbert, Ben. 2011. Sony and PlayStation 3 Jailbreaker George Hotz Settle out of Court. *Engadget*, 11 November. Accessed 30 January 2017. www.engadget.com/2011/04/11/sony-and-playstation-3-jailbreaker-george-hotz-settle-out-of-cou/.

Golding, Dan. 2014. The End of Gamers. *Dan Golding blog*, 28 August. Accessed 30 January 2017. http://dangolding.tumblr.com/post/95985875943/the-end-of-gamers.

Groklaw. 2011. What's Happening in the Class Action Against Sony About Removing OtherOS? – Updated 2Xs. *Groklaw*, 21 February. Accessed 30 January 2017. http://groklaw.net/article.php?story=20110218181557455.

Grusin, Richard. 2010. *Premediation: Affect and Mediality After 9/11*. London: Palgrave Macmillan.

Grusin, Richard. 2015. Radical Mediation. *Critical Inquiry* 42 (1): 124–48. Accessed 30 January 2017. www.jstor.org/stable/10.1086/682998?origin=JSTOR-pdf.

Guevara-Villalobos, Orlando. 2015. Independent Gamework and Identity: Problems and Subjective Nuances. In *DiGRA '15 – Proceedings of the 2015 DiGRA International Conference*, Digital Games Research Association, May, vol. 12.

Guins, Raiford. 2014. *Game After: A Cultural Study of Video Game Afterlife*. Cambridge, MA: The MIT Press.

Hall, Gary. 2009. Introduction: Pirate Philosophy. *Culture Machine* 10: 1–5. Accessed 30 January 2017. http://culturemachine.net/index.php/cm/article/view/367/374.

Haraway, Donna. 1991. A Cyborg Manifesto: Science, Technology, and Socialist-Feminism in the Late Twentieth Century. In *Simians, Cyborgs and Women: The Reinvention of Nature*, 149–81. New York: Routledge.

Haraway, Donna. 2004. Cyborgs to Companion Species: Reconfiguring Kinship in Technoscience. In *The Haraway Reader*, 295–320. New York: Routledge.

Haraway, Donna. 2011. SF: Science Fiction, Speculative Fabulation, String Figures, So Far. Pilgrim Award Acceptance Talk Presented at the Science Fiction Research Association (SFRA) Conference, Lublin, Poland, July. Accessed 3 May 2017. https://people.ucsc.edu/~haraway/Files/PilgrimAcceptanceHaraway.pdf.

Haraway, Donna. 2015. Anthropocene, Capitalocene, Plantationocene, Chthulucene: Making Kin. *Environmental Humanities* 6: 159–65. Accessed 30 January 2017. doi:10.1215/22011919-3615934.

Hayles, Katherine N. 1996. Narratives of Artificial Life. In *Future Natural: Nature, Science, Culture*, edited by George Robertson, Melinda Mash, Lisa Tickner, Jon Bird, Barry Curtis and Tim Putnam, 146–64. London: Routledge.

Heidegger, Martin. 1971a. Building Dwelling Thinking. In *Poetry, Language Thought*, 141–60. New York: Harper & Row.

Heidegger, Martin. 1971b. The Thing. In *Poetry, Language, Thought*, 161–84. New York: Harper & Row.

Herz, Jessie Cameron. 1997. *Joystick Nation: How Videogames Ate Our Quarters, Won Our Hearts, and Rewired Our Minds*. London: Abacus.

Hesmondhalgh, David. 2013. *The Cultural Industries*. 3rd Edition. London: Sage.

Huhtamo, Erkki. 2005. Slots of Fun, Slots of Trouble: An Archaeology of Arcade Gaming. In *Handbook of Computer Games Studies*, edited by Joost Raessens and Jeffrey Goldstein: 3–22. Cambridge, MA: The MIT Press.

Huhtamo, Erkki, and Jussi Parikka. 2011. *Media Archaeology: Approaches, Applications and Implications*. Berkeley, CA: University of California Press.

IndieCade. 2012. Eric Zimmerman – Being a Game Designer: Principles for a Thoughtful Practice – IndieCade 2012. *YouTube*, 19 May 2014. Accessed 30 January 2017. www.youtube.com/watch?v=ba_0pLeAQQ8.

Indie Game: The Movie. 2012. Directed by James Swirsky and Lisanne Pajot.

Ingold, Tim. 2010. Bringing Things to Life: Creative Entanglements in a World of Materials. In *ESRC National Centre for Research Methods*. Accessed 30 January 2017. http://eprints.ncrm.ac.uk/1306/1/0510_creative_entanglements.pdf.

Ingold, Tim. 2011. *Being Alive: Essays on Movement, Knowledge, Description*. London: Routledge.

Jayanth, Meg. 2014. 52% of Gamers Are Women – But the Industry Doesn't Know It. *The Guardian*, 18 September. Accessed 30 January 2017. www.theguardian.com/commentisfree/2014/sep/18/52-percent-people-playing-games-women-industry-doesnt-know.

Juul, Jesper. 2010. *A Casual Revolution: Reinventing Video Games and Their Players*. Cambridge, MA: The MIT Press.

Juul, Jesper. 2014. High-Tech Low-Tech Authenticity: The Creation of Independent Style at the Independent Games Festival. *Proceedings of the 9th International Conference on the Foundations of Digital Games*. Accessed 30 January 2017. www.jesperjuul.net/text/independentstyle/independentstyle.pdf.

JWT Dubai. 2013. App Tycoon. Accessed 30 January 2017. www.jwt.com/en/dubai/work/hsbcapptycoon/.

Kember, Sarah, and Joanna Zylinska. 2012. *Life after New Media: Mediation as a Vital Process*. Cambridge, MA: The MIT Press.

Kent, Steven L. 2001. *The Ultimate History of Videogames*. Roseville, CA: Prima Life.

Kerr, Aphra. 2006. *The Business and Culture of Digital Games. GameWork/Gameplay*. London: Sage.

koyima. 2015. Post on People Are Now Claiming That GamerGate Is Killing Gaming Archiving. *Reddit*, 10 March. Accessed 30 January 2017. www.reddit.com/r/KotakuInAction/comments/2ygk0q/people_are_now_claiming_that_gamergate_is_killing/cpa6sjh.

Krapp, Peter. 2011. *Noise Channels: Glitch and Error in Digital Culture*. Minneapolis, MN: University of Minnesota Press.

Krotoski, Aleks. 2008. Little Big Planet Signals the Start of 'Game3.0'. *The Guardian*, 6 November. Accessed 30 January 2017. www.theguardian.com/technology/2008/nov/06/little-big-planet-lbp-indiegames-games.

Kuchera, Ben. 2011. Donations Pour in for PS3 Hacker. *Wired*, 22 February. Accessed 23 April 2017. www.wired.com/2011/02/hotz-donations/.

Kushner, David. 2011. How Sony's Antipiracy Approach Made It a Hacker Target. *IEEE Spectrum*. Accessed 30 January 2017. http://spectrum.ieee.org/consumer-electronics/gaming/how-sonys-antipiracy-approach-made-it-a-hacker-target/2.

Laclau, Ernesto. 1990. *New Reflections on the Revolution of Our Time*. London: Verso.

Laclau, Ernesto. 1993. Power and Representation. In *Politics, Theory and Contemporary Culture*, edited by Mark Poster. New York: Columbia University Press.

Laclau, Ernesto. 1996. *Emancipation(s)*. London: Verso.

Latour, Bruno. 1999. On Recalling ANT. In *Actor Network Theory and After*, edited by John Law and John Hassard, 15–25. Oxford: Blackwell.

Latour, Bruno. 2005. *Reassembling the Social: An Introduction to Actor-Network-Theory*. Oxford: Oxford University Press.

Latour, Bruno. 2014. Agency at the Time of the Anthropocene. *New Literary History* 18: 1–18. Accessed 30 January 2017. www.bruno-latour.fr/sites/default/files/128-FELSKI-HOLBERG-NLH-FINAL.pdf.

Law, John. 1999. After ANT: Complexity, Naming and Topology. In *Actor Network Theory and After*, edited by John Law and John Hassard, 1–14. Oxford: Blackwell.

Lee, Jesse. 2011. President Obama Talks Education in Boston: 'A Moral and Economic Imperative to Give Every Child the Chance to Succeed'. *The White House*, 8 March. Accessed 30 January 2017. www.whitehouse.gov/blog/2011/03/08/president-obama-talks-education-boston-moral-and-economic-imperative-give-every-chil.

Levy, Steven. 2010. *Hackers: Heroes of the Computer Revolution*. Sebastopol, CA: O'Reilly Media.

Lipkin, Nadav. 2013. Examining Indie's Independence: The Meaning of 'Indie' Games, the Politics of Production, and Mainstream Cooptation. *Loading. . .* 7 (11): 8–24. Edited by Bart Simon. Accessed 30 January 2017. http://journals.sfu.ca/loading/index.php/loading/article/view/122/149.

Makuch, Eddie. 2014a. Percentage of Female Developers Has More Than Doubled Since 2009. *Gamespot*, 24 June. Accessed 30 January 2017. www.gamespot.com/articles/percentage-of-female-developers-has-more-than-doubled-since-2009/1100-6420680/.

Makuch, Eddie. 2014b. EA, Ubisoft, Activision On Why There Are So Few Female Video Game Protagonists. *Gamespot*, 20 June. Accessed 30 January 2017. www.gamespot.com/articles/ea-ubisoft-activision-on-why-there-are-so-few-female-video-game-protagonists/1100-6420600/.

Martin, Bowen C., and Mark Deuze. 2009. The Independent Production of Culture: A Digital Games Case Studies. *Games and Culture* 4 (3): 276–95. Accessed 30 January 2017. doi:10.1177/1555412009339732.

Martin, Michael. 2016. Hacked PS4 Plays Pokémon. *IGN UK*. 4 January. Accessed 30 January 2017. http://uk.ign.com/articles/2016/01/04/hacked-ps4-plays-pokemon.

McGonigal, Jane. 2010. Gaming Can Make a Better World. *TED Ideas Worth Spreading*, February 2010. Accessed 30 January 2017. www.ted.com/talks/jane_mcgonigal_gaming_can_make_a_better_world?language=en.

McGonigal, Jane. 2011. *Reality Is Broken: Why Games Make Us Better and How They Can Change the World*. London: Jonathan Cape.

McLuhan, Marshall. 1964. *Understanding Media: The Extensions of Man*. Cambridge, MA: The MIT Press.

McRobbie, Angela. 2001. 'Everyone Is Creative': Artists as New Economy Pioneers? *OpenDemocracy*, 30 August. Accessed 30 January 2017. www.opendemocracy.net/node/652.

McRobbie, Angela. 2016. *Be Creative: Making a Living in the New Culture Industries*. Cambridge: Polity Press.

McShea, Tom. 2014. We Named the Dog Indie. *Gamespot.com*. 10 July. Accessed 30 January 2017. www.gamespot.com/articles/its-impossible-to-define-indie-so-we-should-stop-u/1100-6420984/.

Michael, Mike. 2000. *Reconnecting Culture, Technology and Nature From Society to Heterogeneity*. London and New York: Routledge.

Molleindustria. 2016. Molleindustria: Radical Games Against the Tyranny of Entertainment. Accessed 30 January 2017. www.molleindustria.org/.

Montfort, Nick, and Ian Bogost. 2009. Platform Studies: Frequently Questioned Answers. *Proceedings of Digital Arts and Culture Conference*. Accessed 30 January 2017. http://nickm.com/if/bogost_montfort_dac_2009.pdf.

Morris, Chris. 2011. Sony: PlayStation Breach Involves 70 million Subscribers *CNBC*, 26 April. Accessed 30 January 2017. www.cnbc.com/id/42769019.

Movel, Michael. 2012. Marketing: Using Your Strengths as an Indie. 11 July. Presentation at *Develop Conference Indie Day*, Brighton, United Kingdom.

Murray, Laura J. 2009. RiP: A Remix Manifesto. Review of *RiP: A Remix Manifesto*, by Brett Gaylor. *Culture Machine* 10: 1–8. Accessed 30 January 2017. www.culturemachine.net/index.php/cm/article/view/372/380.

Newhouse, Alex. 2014. There Is No Other Word to Describe These Games. *Gamespot*. 15 July. Accessed 30 January 2017. www.gamespot.com/articles/dont-throw-indie-away-just-yet-we-still-need-it/1100-6421044/.

Nooney, Laine. 2013. A Pedestal, a Table, a Loveletter: Archaeologies of Gender in Video Game History. *GameStudies* 13 (2). Accessed 30 January 2017. http://gamestudies.org/1302/articles/nooney.

Orland, Kyle. 2014. Digging Up Meaning from the Rubble of an Excavated Atari Landfill. *Ars Technica*, 27 April. Accessed 30 January 2017. http://arstechnica.com/gaming/2014/04/digging-up-meaning-from-the-rubble-of-an-excavated-atari-landfill/.

Orland, Kyle. 2016. Throwing Cold Water on Some of Pokémon Go's Hottest Takes. *Ars Technica UK*, 11 July. Accessed 30 January 2017. http://arstechnica.co.uk/gaming/2016/07/how-successful-is-pokemon-go-really/.

Parikka, Jussi. 2012. *What Is Media Archaeology?* Cambridge: Polity Press.

Parikka, Jussi, and Jaakko Suominen. 2006. Victorian Snakes? Towards a Cultural History of Mobile Games and the Experience of Movement. *Game Studies* 6 (1). Accessed 30 January 2017. http://gamestudies.org/0601/articles/parikka_suominen.

Pedercini, Paolo. 2012. Toward Independence – Indiecade 2012. *Molleindustria.org*. Accessed 30 January 2017. www.molleindustria.org/blog/toward-independence-indiecade-2012-microtalk/.

Poole, Steven. 2000. *Trigger Happy: The Inner Life of Videogames*. London: Fourth Estate.

Pope, Travis. 2016. Pokémon Go Updates: Here Is What We Know Is Coming Next. *Gotta Be Mobile*, 11 July. Accessed 30 January 2017. www.gottabemobile.com/2016/07/11/pokemon-go-updates-here-is-what-we-know-is-coming-next/.

Postman, Neil. 1992. *Technopoly: The Surrender of Culture to Technology*. New York: Knopf.

Press Association. 2016. Oliver Stone Links Pokémon Go to Totalitarianism During Privacy Debate. *The Guardian*, 22 July. Accessed 30 January 2017. www.theguardian.com/technology/2016/jul/22/oliver-stone-links-pokemon-go-to-totalitarianism-during-privacy-debate.

Procter, Lewie. 2012. Cactus on Hotline Miami: 'I'm pretty tired of crappy games that don't really want to do anything special'. *PCGamesN*. Accessed 30 January 2017. www.pcgamesn.com/indie/cactus-hotline-miami-im-pretty-tired-crappy-games-dont-really-want-do-anything-special.

ProPublica. 2013. NSA Documents on Games and Virtual Worlds. *ProPublica*. Accessed 30 January 2017. www.propublica.org/documents/item/889134-games.

Radd, David. 2007. Gaming 3.0: Sony's Phil Harrison Explains the PS3 Virtual Community, Home. *Bloomberg Business Week*, 9 March. Accessed 30 January 2017. www.businessweek.com/stories/2007-03-09/gaming-3-dot-0businessweek-business-news-stock-market-and-financial-advice.

Raessens, Joost. 2014. The Ludification of Culture. In *Rethinking Gamification*, edited by Mathias Fuchs, Sonia Fizek, Paolo Ruffino and Niklas Schrape, 91–118. Lueneburg: Meson Press.

Robarge, Drew. 2014. From Landfill to Smithsonian Collections: 'E.T. the Extra-Terrestrial' Atari 2600 Game. *Smithsonian*, 15 December. Accessed 30 January 2017. http://americanhistory. si.edu/blog/landfill-smithsonian-collections-et-extra-terrestrial-atari-2600-game.

Romano, Aja. 2016. Pokémon Go Might Kill You. Here Is How. *Vox Culture*, 14 July. Accessed 30 January 2017. www.vox.com/2016/7/14/12167088/pokemon-go-societal-breakdown-chaos-explained.

Ruffino, Paolo. 2012. A Theory of Non-Existent Video Games: Semiotic and Video Game Theory. In *Computer Games and New Media Cultures: A Handbook of Digital Game Studies*, edited by Johannes Fromme and Alexander Unger, 107–24. Dordrecht: Springer.

Ruffino, Paolo. 2015. *When One Is Too Many: Molleindustria and Paolo Pedercini*. Ljubljana: Aksioma – Institute for Contemporary Art.

Ryder, April. 2016. Pokémon Go Players Find Mental Health Implications Are Groundbreaking. *Inquisitr News Worth Sharing*, 30 July. Accessed 30 January 2017. www. inquisitr.com/3365757/pokemon-go-mental-health-implications-are-groundbreaking/.

Sargon of Akkad. 2014. A Conspiracy Within Gaming #GamerGate #NotYourShield. *YouTube*, 9 September. Accessed 30 January 2017. www.youtube.com/watch?v=yJyU7RSvs_s.

Schehr, Lawrence R. 1982. Translator's Introduction. In *The Parasite* by Michel Serres. Baltimore, MD: The Johns Hopkins University Press.

Schiesel, Seth. 2011. PlayStation Security Breach a Test of Consumer's Trust. *The New York Times*, 27 April. Accessed 30 January 2017. www.nytimes.com/2011/04/28/arts/video-games/sony-playstation-security-flaw-tests-consumer-trust.html.

Schofield, Jack. 2011. Which Is the Best Format for Ebooks? *The Guardian*, 15 September. Accessed 30 January 2017. www.theguardian.com/technology/askjack/2011/sep/15/ebook-format-drm-kindle.

Schrape, Niklas. 2014. Gamification and Governmentality. In *Rethinking Gamification*, edited by Mathias Fuchs, Sonia Fizek, Paolo Ruffino and Niklas Schrape, 21–46. Lueneburg: Meson Press.

Sennett, Richard. 2008. *The Craftsman*. London: Allen Lane.

Serhan, Yasmeen. 2016. The Health Risks of Pokémon Go. *The Atlantic*, 25 July. Accessed 30 January 2017. www.theatlantic.com/news/archive/2016/07/pokemon-go-health-warning/492899/.

Serres, Michel. 1982. *The Parasite*. Baltimore, MD: The Johns Hopkins University Press.

Serres, Michel, and Bruno Latour. 1995. *Conversations on Science, Culture and Time*. Ann Arbor, MI: The University of Michigan Press.

Seybold, Patrick. 2010. PS3 Firmware (V3.21) Update. *PlayStation Blog*, 28 March. Accessed 30 January 2017. http://blog.us.playstation.com/2010/03/28/ps3-firmware-v3-21-update.

Sinclair, Brendan. 2016a. Indie Acclaim Is 'Like a Drug'. *Gamesindustry. biz*, 31 March. Accessed 30 January 2017. www.gamesindustry.biz/articles/ 2016-03-31-indie-acclaim-is-life-a-drug.

Sinclair, Brendan. 2016b. Life as an Indie: Obscurity, Triage and Trust Issues. *Gamesindustry.biz*, 7 April. Accessed 30 January 2017. www.gamesindustry.biz/articles/ 2016-04-07-life-as-an-indie-obscurity-triage-and-trust-issues.

Standage, Tom. 1999. *The Victorian Internet: The Remarkable Story of the Telegraph and the Nineteenth Century's Online Pioneers*. London: Phoenix.

Stone, Brad. 2009. Amazon Erases Orwell Books from Kindle. *The New York Times*, 17 July. Accessed 30 January 2017. www.nytimes.com/2009/07/18/technology/companies/ 18amazon.html.

Stuart, Keith. 2012. Video Game Tax Breaks: What Does It Mean and What Happens Now? *The Guardian*, 23 March. Accessed 30 January 2017. www.theguardian.com/technology/ gamesblog/2012/mar/23/video-game-tax-credits.

Suominen, Jaakko. 2016. How to Present the History of Digital Games: Enthusiast, Emancipatory, Genealogical, and Pathological Approaches. *Games and Culture* 20 June. doi:10.1177/1555412016653341.

Tazzioli, Martina, Sophie Fuggle, and Yari Lanci. 2015. Introduction. In *Foucault and the History of the Present*, edited by Sophie Fuggle, Yari Lanci and Martina Tazzioli, 1–12. London: Palgrave Macmillan.

This Is Nike+ FuelBand. 2013. Produced by Nike, Inc. Accessed 30 January 2017. www. youtube.com/watch?v=bvMohoDFZ30.

Van Loon, Joost. 2008. *Media Technology: Critical Perspectives*. Maidenhead: McGraw Hill/ Open University Press.

Werbach, Kevin, and Dan Hunter. 2012. *For the Win: How Game Thinking Can Revolutionize Your Business*. Philadelphia, PA: Wharton Digital Press.

Whitson, Jennifer R. 2015. Foucault's FitBit: Governance and Gamification. In *The Gameful World: Approaches, Issues, Applications*, edited by Steffen P. Walz and Sebastian Deterding, 339–58. Cambridge, MA: The MIT Press.

Whitson, Jennifer R., and Bart Simon. 2014. Game Studies Meets Surveillance Studies at the Edge of Digital Culture: An Introduction to a Special Issue on Surveillance, Games and Play. *Surveillance and Society* 12 (3): 309–19. Accessed 30 January 2017. http://ojs.library. queensu.ca/index.php/surveillance-and-society/article/view/games_editorial/games_ed.

Wilson, Andrew G. 2014. A to Z: A DiGRA Letter Series – Part 4. *Silverstring Media Blog*, 20 August. Accessed 30 January 2017. http://archive.li/2UtHJ.

Wolf, Mark J. P. 2012. *Before the Crash: Early Video Game History*. Detroit, MI: Wayne State University Press.

Zerilli, Laura M. G. 2006. This Universalism Which Is Not One. In *Laclau: A Critical Reader*, edited by Simon Critchley and Oliver Marchart, 88–109. London and New York: Routledge.

Zichermann, Gabe, and Christopher Cunningham. 2011. *Gamification by Design: Implementing Game Mechanics in Web and Mobile Apps*. New York: O'Reilly Media.

Zimmerman, Eric. 2002. Do Independent Games Exist? Accessed 30 January 2017. www.ericzimmerman.com/texts/indiegames.html.

Zylinska, Joanna. 2005. *The Ethics of Cultural Studies*. London and New York: Continuum.

Zylinska, Joanna. 2009. *Bioethics in the Age of New Media*. Cambridge, MA: The MIT Press.

Index

Future Media series

Anti-TED thinking for media and technological futures

Goldsmiths Press Future Media series encourages authors to offer a relatively short, sharp intervention in response to actual or potential short-term, utilitarian and instrumentalist thinking about a particular scenario or performance of media and technological futurism.

Our emphasis on feminist, queer, trans, anti racist and/or speculative approaches to media and technological futures calls for alternatives to TED thinking.

The ideas that the Future Media series sees as worth spreading are those that are not solution but problem oriented. Rather than offering instant gratification or short-term utility they are oriented toward complexity and a processual, dynamic environment of co-constituted technologies and users that is not-yet and never fully known. Ideas worth spreading offer a different kind of enchantment, one produced by a question with no easy, obvious, off-the-peg answer.

They are properly theoretical, philosophical, speculative and characterized by imagination, thought-experiments, figures of speech and hypotheses.

The Future Media series will attempt to capture speculative thinking-in-action by incorporating, where appropriate, 'grey literature' such as briefs, sketchbooks and blogposts as well as familiar provisional formats such as the manual and manifesto. Authors are encouraged to reflect on how they are writing as well as what they are writing about and are free to explore modes of communication that are engaging and apposite to our goal of contesting the future.

Books in the series may be single or co-authored, between 45–65,000 words and will be available in digital and print formats.

www.gold.ac.uk/goldsmiths-press   Goldsmiths Press